THE POCKET GUIDE
TO
SPIRITS & LIQUEURS

**Emanuel and
Madeline Greenberg**

**To
D.P.G.
A kindred spirit**

Emanuel and Madeline Greenberg are freelance journalists specializing in spirits, wine, and food. Emanuel has been *Playboy*'s writer on these subjects for more than a decade, and a contributor to the magazine's special editions. Together, the Greenbergs write for a variety of publications—*Harper's Bazaar, Travel & Leisure, Diversion, East/West Network,* and many more. Their books include *Whiskey in the Kitchen, Guide to Wine Drinks,* and *Guide to Flambéing Desserts.* They are also consultants on wine and spirits matters to a number of companies, and travel extensively to wine- and spirit-producing regions in the United States and Europe to sniff out the latest trends and developments. Both are members of the New York Wine Writers Circle, and of several wine and spirit societies.

The Pocket Guide to

Spirits & Liqueurs

Emanuel & Madeline Greenberg

A Perigee Book

Perigee Books
are published by
The Putnam Publishing Group
200 Madison Avenue
New York, New York 10016

A Quarto Book

Library of Congress Cataloging in Publication Data
Greenberg, Emanuel.
The pocket guide to spirits and liqueurs.

"A Perigee book."
1. Liquors.   2. Liqueurs.   I. Greenberg, Madeline.
II. Title.
TP597.G73 1983   641.2′ 5   82-20532

ISBN 0-399-50730-2

First Perigee Printing, 1983
The Pocket Guide to Spirits & Liqueurs
was produced and prepared by
Quarto Marketing, Ltd.
212 Fifth Avenue,
New York, New York 10010

Editor: **Gene Santoro**
Designer: **Richard Boddy**
Illustrations: **Edgar Blakeney**

Typeset by BPE Graphics, Inc.
Printed and bound in the United States of America by
Maple-Vail Group.

CONTENTS

Acknowledgements

We called on many individuals and organizations with background in the liquor industry for information and counsel in the preparation of this book - and we thank them all. We're especially grateful to the following, and particularly to Russell W. McLauchlan, Vice President of Quality Control, Jos. E. Seagram & Sons, Inc., for his unfailing patience and sagacity.

Charles Angelini
Jean-Marie Beulque
Bureau National Interprofessionnel de l'Armagnac
Bureau National Interprofessionnel du Cognac
California Brandy Advisory Board
Jean Danflou
Robert Gilbert
Nancy Glaser
Michael Goldstein
Dan Hecht
Glen Heller
William Houlton
Hans Jost
Earl La Roe
Gustave Ledun
Jack MacGowan
Andy McElhone
James R. McManus
Anita Mizener
Dr. Lucien Rose
Dr. G. Joseph Servadio

Introduction

Spirit: A distilled alcoholic beverage. This cryptic
dictionary definition of the word "spirit" gives little inkling
of the vast array and variety of potable products it covers.
The term encompasses liqueurs as well as whiskies, brandies, vodkas, gins, rums, tequilas, and more—plus esoter-
ica from arak to zubrowka. Note, however, that it does *not*
include wine or beer—alcoholic beverages that are derived
through the process of fermentation.

Modern spirits have developed through a long process of
evolution. As far back as the fourth century B.C., Aristotle
suggested the *possibility* of spirits when he wrote: "Seawa-
ter can be made potable by distillation; wine and other
liquids can be submitted to the same process." But this
enormous insight does not seem to have been pursued
until the eighth or ninth century A.D., when Arab alchemists devised the alembic in an effort to obtain finer
essences for perfumes. They also used this crude apparatus
to distill alcohol, although not to create a potable spirit: The
intent was to discover a way to convert base metal into
gold, or to find a universal cure for disease—both laudable
objectives.

As knowledge of the process spread through Europe, the
new practitioners had similar hopes for the potent liquid.
They called it *aqua vitae* or *eau de vie*—water of life—an

expression of their faith in its powers. The base metal-into-gold dream remained just that, and even though the hope for a universal panacea was never fulfilled, spirits *were* discovered to have some therapeutic qualities. Patients who were treated with these early spirit nostrums found they induced a feeling of relaxation and well-being. From there, it was just a short segue to their use in social situations and, simply, as refreshment beverages.

From its Beginning, with the primitive distillates of the alchemists and pharmacists, the world of spirits has continued to grow and expand, as a seemingly endless and bewildering flow of new items, and variations on old themes, enter the market place. Nevertheless, almost all spirits can be broadly classified into half a dozen basic—and not difficult to comprehend—categories.

The purpose of this concise *Guide* is to familiarize you with the rich variety of spirits now available on liquor shop shelves, and to enhance the pleasure and satisfaction you derive from them. In the process, we hope to answer questions that have puzzled you; clear up misconceptions, misunderstandings, and myths; interest you in engaging new taste experiences; and generally help you to become the kind of consumer who unerringly makes the most satisfying choices when shopping for spirits. It is neither our intention nor our function to impose personal opinions or judgments on the reader. Quite the contrary; our objective is to liberate the casual bibber from the tyranny of arbitrary pronouncements by self-styled "experts" and thus allow individual preferences to come into play. To this end, we have included clear, illuminating material on the *theme* of spirits along with candid shopping information and advice.

First—and just for fun—test your present knowledge of spirits by running through the quiz on page 140. Then, take the quiz again in about 6 months. You will be surprised at how much authority you have acquired in the interim.

How To Use This Book

This *Guide* deals with the essential spirit categories and their sub-groups, classified according to country of origin and style. Each chapter begins with a short description of the nature of the spirit, its history, and how it is formulated. The major portion of the chapter is devoted to an *Insider's Guide*, which details the overall organoleptic, or sensory, qualities of the spirit and how these relate to its uses. Tips on gleaning information from labels are also given. This is followed by an extensive list of individual brands that indicates the range of quality and the overt or subtle taste characteristics of each. Where there are no meaningful differences within a category, that fact has been pointed out. These observations are, of course, our subjective perceptions, and they may not match yours precisely. At the very least, however, they indicate that there are stylistic and quality differences between Brand X and Brand Y. With that insight, you can make a more informed decision as to which might give you greater pleasure.

Each *Insider's Guide* concludes with an *Application* section—how to use the particular spirit to best advantage. We consider this to be essential information for any intelligent buying, serving, and appreciation of spirits. It makes no sense to pour a spirit costing ten dollars when a five dollar one will do as well. On the other hand, it could be disappointing, or embarrassing, to use grade B goods when grade A is called for. Vodka is an instructive example: For mixed drinks, the exceptionally clean U.S. vodkas are preferable to the much more costly European vodkas, but if you sip vodka neat, the distinctive European examples *are* worth the difference in price.

In describing the production and character of spirits, there are certain terms that appear again and again. For quick reference, they are defined in the *Basic Spirit Vocabulary* on page 11. It should also be noted that detailed descriptions of the various stages in the production of a spirit are given in the Whisky and Brandy chapters. These descriptions apply one way or another to the other spirits discussed in this *Guide*. Needless repetition would serve no purpose.

Basic Spirit Vocabulary

AGING: The process of storing spirits in wood (usually oak) casks or barrels to help them mature. The spirit interacts with the wood, drawing flavor and color from it. The porousness of the wood allows air and moisture to enter and leave the barrels, further affecting the development of the spirit into a rounded, mellow beverage. Once the spirit is bottled, however, it will not change appreciably as long as the container remains airtight.

ALCOHOL: A colorless, volatile liquid derived through *FERMENTATION* or *DISTILLATION* (which see).

ALEMBIC: See *STILL.*

BLENDING: The process of mixing different batches of spirits together to achieve a balanced product that is usually better than any of its parts. Blending also helps to maintain a consistent style year to year. Blending sometimes involves mixing different types of spirits, and sometimes mixing spirits of the same type but differing in age or handling.

BODY: The perception of weight or density; a mouth-filling quality. Usually implies approval.

CARAMEL: Burnt sugar added to spirits in minute quantities to impart color. Though derived from sugar, it is not sweet.

COFFEY STILL: See *STILL.*

CONGENERS: By-products or impurities that are produced, along with alcohol, during *FERMENTATION* and

DISTILLATION (which see). Congeners are of a varied nature, but a number contribute important flavor elements to alcoholic beverages.

COOPERAGE: Barrels, casks, and other wooden containers used for aging and storing spirits.

DELIMITED: A word applied to a geographic area, with specified borders, within which a particular spirit may be legally made.

DISTILLATE: The concentrated liquid obtained from *DISTILLATION* (which see).

DISTILLATION: A process that uses heat to extract the alcohol from a liquid that contains both alcohol and water. It is possible because alcohol vaporizes at 172.4°F. and water vaporizes at 212°F. Thus, when an alcoholic liquid is heated, the alcohol turns into a gas and rises, leaving the water behind. As these gaseous vapors cool, they condense back into liquid form, becoming concentrated alcoholic beverages, or spirits. This process takes place in an apparatus called a *STILL* (which see).

ETHYL ALCOHOL: A potable alcohol found in alcoholic beverages.

FEINTS: The first and last of the *DISTILLATE* to come off the still. Because they contain a high percentage of impurities, they are set apart from the main body of the *DISTILLATE,* and are redistilled later.

FERMENTATION: A step, prior to distillation, during which a mash comprised of crushed grain with water, grapes, sugar cane, etc., is injected with yeasts. The yeasts convert the sugar into ethyl alcohol and carbon dioxide gas. The gas drifts off, and the remaining mixture contains a fairly low level of alcohol, which can be extracted and concentrated through distillation. Potable spirits can be derived from any plant or plant product containing either fermentable sugars or starch that can be converted to such sugars.

FINISH: The lingering taste or aftertaste left on the palate.

FORESHOT A term sometimes used to describe the first fraction of the *FEINTS* (which see).

HEADS AND TAILS: Another name for *FORESHOTS* and *FEINTS* (which see).

LIQUOR: A distilled alcoholic beverage; an alternate term for "spirit."

NEAT: Spirits as poured from the bottle, without ice or mixer.

NEUTRAL SPIRITS: Spirits distilled, from any organic

substance, at or above 190 *PROOF* (which see). Because they are almost pure alcohol, neutral spirits lack *distinctive* character, taste, or odor.

PATENT STILL: See *STILL.*

POTABLE: Drinkable.

PRIVATE LABEL: A shop's own label, usually the store name, on a particular item or line of spirits. Often good values, they are not always consistent, shipment to shipment. If you find one that pleases you, and the price is right, order a supply of that label from the same outlet.

PROOF: A term used for indicating the alcoholic content of a spirit. It's measured with a device called a hydrometer. The term originated before there was precise instrumentation for determining alcoholic content. During that period, a small quantity of spirit would be mixed with gunpowder, and ignited: If the mixture burned with a steady blue flame, this was "proof" that it contained the proper amount of alcohol—approximately 50% by volume. The degree symbol (°) is used for proof. There are 3 systems for indicating proof or alcohol content:

UNITED STATES: Proof is double the percentage of alcohol in a spirit. Thus, a whiskey labeled 100° contains 50% alcohol by volume.

UNITED KINGDOM: Proof is based on a formula developed by Bartholomew Sykes in the early 19th century, according to which a whisky labeled 100° U.K. contains 57.1% alcohol by volume. Spirits containing more than 57.1% alcohol are "overproof," those with less are "underproof."

EUROPEAN: The actual percentage of alcohol by volume is shown on the label. This is called the *Gay-Lussac* (GL) system, for the French chemist who introduced it.

Spirits for export are labeled as to alcohol content according to the system used in the country of destination. The proof of a given type of brand or spirits is not always the same; it may vary from country to country, and from state to state in the U.S. However, the proof or percentage of alcohol is always indicated on the label.

The U.K. proof designation is now being phased out, to be replaced by GL, in order to conform to the practice of the European Economic Community (EEC) countries. Until the system is in full use, the percentage of alcohol in U.K. proof may be determined by the following formula: U.K. proof x 4 ÷ 7. (Example: 70° U.K. x 4 = 280 ÷ 7 = 40% alcohol) To convert to U.S. Proof, double the percentage of alcohol. To convert U.S. proof to U.K. proof, use the following formula: U.S. proof ÷ 8 x 7. (Example: 80° U.S. ÷ 8 = 10 x 7 = 70° U.K.) For easy conversion, consult the proof equivalency chart below.

NOTE: Only U.S. proof designations are used in this book.

% ALCOHOL (GL)	U.S. PROOF	U.K. PROOF
15	30	26.3
20	40	35
25	50	43.8
30	60	52.5
35	70	61.3
40	80	70
41	82	71.75
42	84	73.5
43	86	75.25
43.4	86.8	76
44	88	77
45	90	78.75
50	100	87.5
55	110	96.3
57	114	100
60	120	105
65	130	113.75
70	140	122.5
75	150	131.25
80	160	140
85	170	148.75
90	180	157.5
95	190	166.25
100	200	175

RECTIFICATION: A term, applied to such aspects of the spirit-making process as blending, coloring, flavoring, or even redistilling, that implies a further treatment of the spirit beyond *DISTILLATION.*

SCHNAPPS/SNAPS: A northern European generic term for alcoholic beverages, especially the clear, unaged spirits such as vodka, gin, and aquavit.

STILL: The apparatus in which *DISTILLATION* takes place. There are two basic types of stills:

1. ***Pot Still*** (sometimes called an *alembic*): This is the most ancient of stills. It comes in a variety of shapes but is basically an oversize kettle, the top of which tapers into a long, curving pipe. The kettle is used for heating the alcoholic liquid; the pipe is used for capturing, cooling, and condensing the vapors into concentrated alcohol. A pot still generally yields a spirit of no more than 140° that contains many congeneric elements.

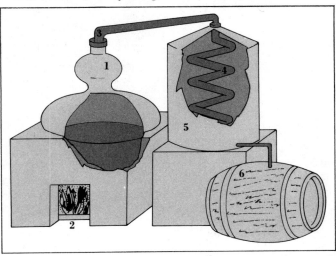

The pot still is a primitive instrument devised to separate the crude alcohol from the water in a spiritous mixture. It is based on the simple principle that alcohol will boil, and vaporize, at a lower temperature than water. This is almost always done in two separate operations, sometimes more. The pots (1) resemble huge, onion-shaped kettles. An alcoholic solution is fed into a kettle and heated (2), which liberates the alcoholic portion in the mixture. These alcoholic gases rise and pass through a narrow pipe (3). The vapors then run through a serpentine coil (4), colloquially termed "the worm." A cold water bath in the worm tub (5) condenses the vapors in the coils, converting them back to liquid form. The first and last portions of the distillation are removed (6) and redistilled. This is particularly true with the second distillation. Only the heart—the main portion of the run—is acceptable in quality establishments.

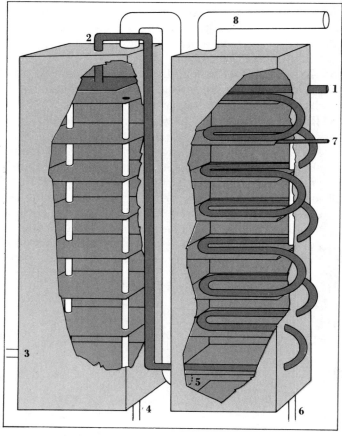

The column still (also called the continuous still) is a technological
advance over the pot still. It is more efficient, requiring only a single
distillation done in one continuous operation. This is not to imply that
it is superior for all purposes.

The still consists of two tall, interconnected columns, each divided
into chambers by horizontal, perforated plates. One column is called
the analyser and the other the rectifier. The alcoholic mixture enters
the rectifier at the inlet (1) and descends via a pipe where it is met by
steam introduced at the base of the column. The heated mixture
crosses over to the analyser column (2). It dribbles down over the
plates, running into a charge of steam (3). The extreme heat separates
out the alcohol and other volatile elements; the watery remains are led
off at the bottom (4). The alcoholic vapors drift back to the base of the
rectifier (5). The vapors rising in the column are cooled by the new
wash running down the pipe. Undesirable elements are taken off at
the base of the column (6). The desirable fraction changes back to a
liquid closer to the top of the rectifier column, and is drawn off (7) at
various stages. Undesirable elements are also removed at the very top
of the column (8), collected, and redistilled.

2. ***Column or Continuous Still:*** This consists of two cylindrical columns fitted with a system of inter-connecting, steam-heated tubes. The alcoholic liquid is fed into the tubes, where it is distilled, redistilled, and finally taken off as a highly concentrated and purified alcohol. The invention of the continuous still is attributed to Aeneas Coffey in 1830. Actually, Coffey patented an improvement on an earlier model invented by Robert Stein, a Scottish distiller. For obvious reasons, the continuous still is sometimes called the *Coffey still* or the *patent still.*

STRAIGHT: Not mixed with another spirit; unblended. In some situations, it means not rectified.

Whisky/
Whiskey

WHISKY/WHISKEY is a spirit made by fermenting and distilling grain, and there is a broad range of examples from many lands.

By long-established custom, Scottish distillers spell the name of the spirit they make from grain *whisky* (pl. *whiskies*), while Irish and U.S. distillers spell their product *whiskey* (pl. *whiskeys*). Distillers in other countries, such as Canada, who make such products usually follow the Scottish spelling. As it happens, the United States government uses the *whisky* spelling throughout its "Standards of Identity for Distilled Spirits," regardless of source. Occasionally a U.S. distiller will do the same, attempting perhaps to suggest that the product is an import when it is not. In this *Guide,* we will use whichever spelling is traditional to the specific item being discussed, but will follow U.S. spelling for general references.

The character of a whisky is determined by such factors as the principal grain or grains in the mash, the type of still used, the details of distillation, the proof at which the spirit runs off the still, the type of cooperage in which it is aged, and the length of aging time. For instance, though bourbon and Scotch are both whiskies, they are unmistakably different from each other. Bourbon, distilled predominantly from corn, leaves a faintly sweet perception on the palate; Scotch, made from barley that has been dried over open peat fires, retains a trace of smokiness in its scent and taste.

There is little doubt that the use of grain as a source of alcohol originated among the Celts in the British Isles. The time is less certain, but appears to be somewhere between the 10th and 15th centuries. The name given the distillate—variously spelled *uisge beatha, uisce beatha, usquebaugh, uisgebaugh,* and pronounced *wee-ska-bah*—meant "water of life." Over the centuries, the word was Anglicized to *whisky* and eventually extended to all spirits distilled from cereals or grains.

HOW WHISKY IS MADE

All whisky making starts by heating a mash of grain in a large vat called a mash tun. When the starches in the grain have been converted into fermentable sugars, the liquid, called the wort, is drawn off and fermented with yeasts. The resultant beer, or wash, is distilled to produce whisky, usually between 140° and 189°, depending on type. With few exceptions, whiskies are aged for a time in oak barrels before bottling. At bottling time, enough water is added to the whisky to reduce it to the desired proof. The color may be rectified with a bit of caramel, as well.

Whiskies are bottled in a range of proofs, from 80° to 114°. At one time, 86°–86.8° was the norm, but in recent years, 80° whiskies have become more prevalent.

The British Isles

The British Isles are represented by two basic types— Scotch whisky from Scotland and Irish whiskey from Ireland. (England produces a number of spirits, described elsewhere, but whisky is not among them.) Both lands claim to be the original source of whisky, but there is little hard evidence as to whether the art of distilling spirits from grain crossed the Irish Sea from west to east or east to west—or precisely when it may have happened. It *is* known that the soldiers of King Henry II of England encountered *uisce beatha* when they invaded Ireland in the 12th century. This precedes the oldest known reference to Scotch whisky, an entry in the Scottish Exchequer Rolls for 1494, which reads "eight bolls of malt to Friar John Cor wherewith to make aquavitae." In any event, there are significant similarities *and* differences between these two whisky types.

Scotland

A Scottish saying has it that "There's whisky and there's guid whisky, but there's nae bad whisky." The whisky in question is the native spirit—what the world outside of Scotland knows as "Scotch." While Scottish whisky production is abundantly regulated as to ingredients and process, geography is the primary criterion for calling a spirit "Scotch." This was settled once and for all in 1909 when a British "Royal Commission on Whisky and other Potable Spirits" declared that a whisky wholly distilled in Scotland was Scotch—and that was that. Other countries have agreed to the principle, and even where there have been attempts to imitate this unique whisky, the end product in such cases has a name other than Scotch.

Whisky making was well established in Scotland by the 16th century, largely as a cottage industry. Farmers reserved a portion of their grain crop to ferment and distill, producing a coarse, harsh whisky. Although it was mostly for their own use, a portion was frequently sold or bartered to friends and neighbors, thus creating the early commercial trade in Scotch. Inevitably, the government sensed the possibility of revenue from this random traffic in spirits, and in 1644 the Scottish parliament imposed its first excise tax on whisky. This, and subsequent taxes,were vigorously resisted by the feisty inhabitants of remote Highland regions, where illicit distillation flourished for almost two hundred years.

Moonshiners, called "smugglers" in Scotland, were resourceful at hiding their activities. Stories are told of stills ensconced in churches to avoid detection, and of whisky shipments transported in funeral corteges. At one point, the government offered a reward to anybody who reported the location of an illegal still. Canny smugglers worked both sides of the fence. They would dismantle a worn-out still, salvaging the usable parts but leaving enough of it in place to show a whisky-making capability. One of their group would then lead the tax collector to the spot and receive his reward. The money would be used to buy new parts, and the still would be reassembled in another glen. Robert Burns expressed the feeling of his countrymen when he sang, "Freedom and whisky gang thegither."

HOW SCOTCH IS MADE

There are two broad categories of Scotch—*malt whisky* and *blended whisky*, the latter a mixture of malt and grain whiskies.

FOOLIN' THE BARLEY

Each grain of barley is an embryo plant, complete in itself. In the spring, when conditions are right, the plant will start to sprout or germinate. In the process, enzymes are developed that convert the starch into sugar, food for the growing plant. But manufacturing Scotch whisky is a year-round operation. So the distiller simulates the conditions of spring in his malt house, moistening and warming the barley, inducing it to sprout and develop maltase, the enzyme that converts the plant's starch to fermentable sugar. Old-time distillery hands in the Scottish Highlands have their own name for this basic procedure. They call it "foolin' the barley."

Malt Scotch

This is the original Scotch, the authentic *usquebaugh*. Its sole ingredient is malted (sprouted) barley, preferably—but not necessarily—grown in Scotland. The malt is first dried on wire screens over peat fires. The acrid smoke filtering through the mesh imparts a distinctive, pungent tang to the malt that carries over into the flavor of the final product.

Scottish distillers attribute great importance to the water they use in the mash, insisting that only the H_2O from local wells and streams will do. But basically, the first steps in making Scotch are not different from those for any other whisky. The wort is fermented into beer or *wash*, which contains about 10% alcohol. The wash goes into a copper pot still, emerging as *low wines*. These go into a second pot still (called the "low wines still") to run off as raw, colorless whisky of about 140°. The first and last distillations, called the *feints*, contain many impurities and are set aside, to be added to a subsequent batch of low wines for redistillation. However, certain that are characteristic of the specific whisky are retained. Called congeners elements, they remain in the "heart" of the distillation to contribute many rich flavor notes.

Pot stills in malt distilleries come in a variety of shapes, and distillers have an almost mystical attachment to their own models—including the effects of wear developed with use. When a part must be replaced, its bumps, dents, and scratches are faithfully reproduced, lest any alteration affect some nuance of the whisky.

After distillation, the new whisky goes into previously used oak casks for aging into the mellow spirit it will eventually become. Old sherry casks are preferred, for the subtleties of color and flavor they impart, but they are not nearly as available as distillers' advertising would lead one to believe. A minimum of three years of wood aging is mandatory before bottling, but malts require longer aging—usually five to seven years. Fifteen years in

SCOTLAND
Malt Whiskey Distilleries

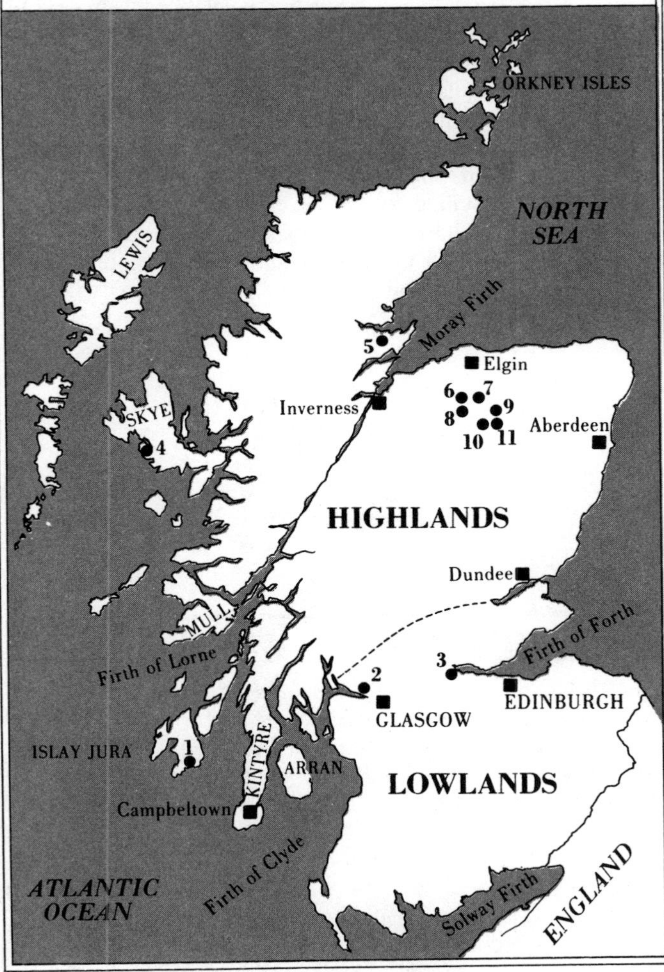

ORKNEY ISLES

NORTH SEA

LEWIS

Moray Firth

5

Elgin

SKYE

6 7

4

8 9

Inverness

10 11

Aberdeen

HIGHLANDS

Dundee

MULL

Firth of Forth

Firth of Lorne

2

3

GLASGOW

EDINBURGH

ISLAY JURA

1

KINTYRE

ARRAN

LOWLANDS

Campbeltown

ATLANTIC OCEAN

Firth of Clyde

Solway Firth

ENGLAND

1. LAPHROAIG	7. MACALLAN
2. AUCHENTOSHAN	8. CARDOW/CARDHU
3. ROSEBANK	9. GLENFIDDICH
4. TALISKER	10. GLENLIVET, THE
5. GLENMORANGIE	11. MORTLACH
6. GLEN GRANT	

Scotland produces much less Malt whisky than grain whisky. The finest single Malts are unquestionably distilled in the Highlands, although other regions also make some malts. The more interesting and important brands of Highland Malt Whiskies are shown on the map, along with two of better Lowland Malt whiskies.

wood is considered the limit for most malts; some even decline after that point, becoming excessively woody. It takes a malt of special character, just as with wine, to benefit from really long aging. In fact, one exporter wryly opined that the ideal aging time for malts was "eight to ten years for palatability...twelve to fifteen years for advertising."

At present, there are well over 100 Scottish malt whiskies, each the product of a single distillery, which is why they are often referred to as "single malts." Nevertheless, despite their number and diversity, malts account for less than half the whisky produced in Scotland. The majority are destined to be mixed with grain whiskies, resulting in the blended product most of us associate with Scotch. Despite the fact that single malts are now more popular than ever, particularly in the United States, *only about 5%* of the total malt whisky production is bottled unblended.

INSIDER'S GUIDE TO MALT SCOTCH

Single malts are the most individualized Scotch whiskies, each having its unique flavor and style. While such production variables as the type of peat, density of smoke, length of drying time, water, qualities, shape of still, cooperage, aging, etc., are all determining factors, the most critical is the area in which the distillery is located.

Malt whiskies are made in four distinct regions of Scotland: the *Highlands*—north of an imaginary line from Dundee in the east to Greenock in the west, including the islands off the mainland; *Islay* (pronounced **Eye**-luh)—the most southerly of Scotland's western isles; the *Lowlands*—south of the Dundee-Greenock line; and *Campbeltown*—on the Kintyre peninsula in southwestern Scotland. Whiskies that are bottled as single malts come primarily from the more than 90 distilleries in the Highlands, with just a few from Islay and the Lowlands. Lowland malts are called "fillers," which describes their general function. The clumsy Campbeltowns are hardly a factor these days; they are used almost exclusively as blending whiskies and are rarely available as single malts.

Although Highland malts cover a spectrum of styles, they are essentially elegant, relatively light, quite fragrant and smooth and range from penetrating and complex to an almost flowery delicacy. Islay, which has 8 distilleries, makes forthright, peaty, pungent malts. Their distinctive character is derived from an extra-heavy peat smoking and from water that comes from streams that flow over peat beds.

 ## MALT SCOTCH BUYING GUIDE

Most malt whiskies are either 86° or 86.8°. The difference is for all practical purposes insignificant.

Highland Malt Whiskies

BRANDS ▶

Cardhu (12 years): One of the lightest of the malts in color and body, yet fairly well-peated; clean; slight sweet edge in finish.

Glenfiddich (10 years): World's most popular bottled malt; lightly fragrant; dryer and not as peaty as The Glenlivet; very clean and well balanced, the one to break in on. Glenfiddich's **Highland Still Master's Crock** (101°) has considerably more depth and authority.

Glen Grant: Comes in a variety of proof and age combinations: Be sure to check specifics on label before purchase; younger bottlings tend to be a little light and gruff.

The Glenlivet (12 years): The first legally licensed distillery in Scotland (1823), and therefore the only one permitted to use the name "Glenlivet" alone, not coupled with another name. (Highland malts made in the Glenlivet vicinity may, if they wish, hyphenate that name with their own. It's more of a marketing ploy than an indication of style or quality.) Definite, but not heavy, body; medium peat and aroma; slightly sweet, fruity nose; clean, very well made.

Glenmorangie (10 years): From the upper Highland region, north of Inverness; delicate flowery fragrance and taste, captivating fruitiness and sweetness in the finish; a charmer.

Macallan (12 years): Mellow, smooth, fairly rich; hits the middle notes; not peaty—an insider's choice.

Mortlach (12 years): Fragrant, round body; lightly peated, complex; finishes soft.

Other Malt Whiskies

BRANDS ▶

Auchentoshan (10 years): Lowland malt; moderately peated, light body, sweet finish.

Laphroig (10 years, 91.4°): Distilled on Islay, this is the lustiest, most distinctive of the malts; very long on peat, plus a whisper of salt and a trace of iodine; has been compared to drinking smoked kippers, but sells well in California, where it has been known to emerge number one in blind tastings of malt Scotches.

Rosebank: Lowland malt; is dryer and more austere than Auchentoshan.

Talisker (12 years): From the Isle of Skye; robust, full-bodied, smooth, and a touch sweet; peaty aftertaste; bridges the ground between Highland and Islay whiskies.

Application: Malt whiskies may be enjoyed neat or with a light splash of cold water "to liberate the bouquet." They have the backbone to stand up to ice. They are also interesting and agreeable in a snifter, after dinner, as an alternative to cognac. With rare exceptions, however, they do not work well in mixed drinks, tending to overwhelm rather than blend with the other ingredients.

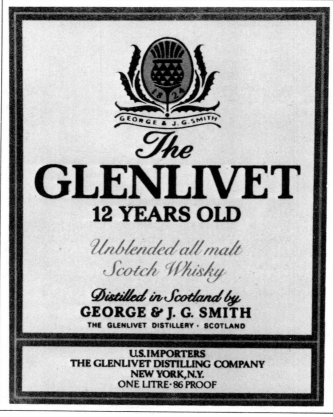

The granddaddy of all branded Scotch whiskey and the only one permitted to use the name "Glenlivet" alone and unhyphenated. Therefore the name, The Glenlivet. This historic association is no guarantee of quality, although it is an excellent product.

Blended Scotch Whisky

This is a mixture of malt and grain whiskies. Grain whisky, a bland spirit, came on the scene with the invention of the patent, or continuous, still in 1830. About 30 years later, a number of distillers, led by Andrew Usher & Co. of Edinburgh, began mixing grain whisky with traditional malt to make a lighter, less aggressive, and less costly Scotch whisky. It was a stunningly successful idea, increasing the acceptance of Scotch, first in Great Britain and eventually in the world. Not coincidentally, it also helped to extend the limited supply of pot still malt whisky.

Grain whisky is made from a mash of several grains—predominantly corn, with small amounts of both malted and unmalted barley. In this instance, however, the barley has *not* been dried over peat smoke. As with malt whisky, the wort is fermented, but the resultant wash is fed into the continuous still, to run off at about 180 proof. Distillation at such high proof eliminates many of the substances that contribute flavor and character to pot still whiskies. The new grain whisky is aged in used oak for the requisite three years, and occasionally longer, but even with aging, grain whiskies are quite bland, almost neutral. Virtually none are bottled unblended.

A measure of the efficiency of the continuous still is that only 14 distilleries currently produce all the grain whisky made in Scotland. Most are in the southern part of the country.

The mystique of Scotch blending rivals that of cognac and champagne. As many as 50 individual whiskies—both malts and grains—can go into a blend. Blenders select their whiskies by nose rather than taste when deciding on the components and proportions to be used. Their trained sniffers adeptly detect both apparent and potential nuances of flavor and style from the aromas of the whiskies they work with. Occasionally, a whisky is selected for the color it will add to the blend.

After the blend has been made, it is left in oak casks for several months to "marry." Before bottling, caramel is usually added to maintain consistency of hue, lot to lot. Note that *there is no legally required percentage of malt whiskies to grain whiskies,* nor do blenders reveal their formulas. And the proportion of malts in some blends is surprisingly modest.

INSIDER'S GUIDE TO
BLENDED SCOTCH

The more malt whiskies in a blend, the smokier and "Scotchier" it tends to taste, although the style of the malts is a factor, too. Most blends, however, contain far more grain than malt whiskies—probably between 60% and 80% of the mix, and occasionally even more. These proportions are as much a response to public taste—which has been leaning to less flavorful spirits, generally—as to economics, malts being far costlier than grain whiskies. An age statement on a bottle of blended Scotch whisky refers to that of the *youngest* whisky in the mix, never to an average. Blended Scotch breaks down into two basic levels: **bulk** and **bottled in Scotland.**

Bulk Scotches

Bulk Scotches are shipped in barrels and bottled at their destination. This method of handling represents a saving to producers and distributors, who imply that this is the reason for the lower price. But it is only one of several factors. The whiskies themselves are usually the younger, lighter, and less complex blends, with the lowest ratio of malt to grain whisky. Nor is the blending as painstaking, which leads to a lack of consistency from batch to batch of some bulk Scotches.

Though there are differences among them, bulk Scotches lack unique style and show the least variation, brand to brand. Overall, they tend to be somewhat listless and a bit thin. However, they represent good value for those who prefer only a touch of smoky Scotch flavor in their whisky or who use them primarily in mixed drinks.

BULK SCOTCH BUYING GUIDE

The label on a bottle of bulk Scotch will usually include the phrase "Distilled and Blended in Scotland." The *absence* of the words "Bottled in Scotland," along with the price, are the buyer's clue to bulk Scotch. Most are bottled at 80°, some are 86°, and a few brands come in both strengths—depending on the market. Check the label.

BRANDS ▶

Clan MacGregor: Exceedingly light; Scotch in name but not in character.

Inver House: Similar to Inver House.

Old Smuggler: Full in flavor but by no means heavy; peaty nose but fades a bit in the mouth.

Passport: One of the fullest the balance of a more expensive blend but lacks the complexity.

Usher's Green Stripe: Medium-full and lightly peated; quite smooth on the tongue.

Vat 69: Similar to Usher's Green Stripe but not as smooth.

Bottled in Scotland

These Scotches (always labeled "Bottled in Scotland") make up about two-thirds of the Scotch market. They are more expensive than bulks, and not just because of the higher production costs involved in filling, labeling, and shipping bottles. The whiskies are older and the blends more carefully selected and maintained. The percentage of malt whiskies is somewhat larger than for the less expensive bulks, and one might think that they would be more intensely flavored. This, however, is not always the case. A number are definitely light on smoky Scotch taste—again, because distillers have responded to the public demand for muted whiskies. In line with that, some producers make a point of keeping the color of their whiskies on the pale side to give the perception of lightness, when in fact the whisky may have fairly generous flavor and medium to full body. One cannot assume that light color is an indication of light body and flavor.

Bottled-in-Scotland whiskies fall into three categories: **Premium, Super-premium,** and **Ultra-premium.**

Premium (sometimes called "standard") Scotch is by far the largest group. It includes the best-known labels, and their character has shaped the public impression of what Scotch is like. Premium Scotches are generally smooth and balanced; even when only mildly peaty, they offer distinct flavor and bouquet, with hints of fruitiness and a scent of grain. All "shipped-in-glass" brands are 86°, except where noted.

Super-premium Scotches are suave bottlings, costlier than premiums but with a difference you can taste. The generous lacing of malt whisky, and the quality of the malts, imparts intensity and a palpable malt tang to the blend. Twelve years or more in the cask round out and mellow the super-premiums, and they flaunt their richness and bouquet.

★ PREMIUM SCOTCH ★
BUYING GUIDE

Several of our perceptions may surprise you, as they did us. Apparently, some brands have tinkered with their formulas, without proclaiming the fact too loudly.

BRANDS ▶

Ballantine's: Light smoky nose, fairly light body, slightly malty and a touch sweet in finish.

Bell's Extra Special: Light peat, medium-light body, dry, a bit flat in mouth.

Cutty Sark: Medium malty/peaty nose; not well balanced, bitterness in finish.

Dewar's White Label: Fairly peaty nose with topnotes of Islay malt, medium body, balanced.

Famous Grouse: Lightly smoky, sweet nose; not much character; was formerly available at 90°.

J&B: Lightly peated; fruity; more body than Ballantine's, surprisingly; slight sweet edge.

Johnnie Walker Red: Quite peaty aroma and flavor; medium-full body; smooth, dry; slight medicinal notes in aftertaste.

Something Special: Something different! Fruity, sweetish, soft nose; very little peat; smooth round body; an atypical Scotch whisky.

White Horse: Fairly full in nose and mouth, some bite, a bit harsh.

★ SUPER-PREMIUM SCOTCH ★
BUYING GUIDE

BRANDS ▶

Chivas Regal: Malty, peaty, complex; medium-full, silky body; no sharp corners; fair amount of peat, but so well-balanced that nothing dominates.

Haig Pinch: Lightly peaty, malty nose; medium bodied, smooth, no special distinction; slightly dank aftertaste; not up to Chivas and Johnnie Walker Black.

Johnnie Walker Black: Heavy color, aroma, and flavor, yet gentle; heavily peated, suggesting Islay malts in the blend.

Ultra-premium Scotches are distillers' show pieces, more like individual gems than a category. The hallmark of this group is age—20 years or more in cask. They are voluptuous and sensuous whiskies of singular finesse and lingering finish. The large proportion of malts in the mixture imparts a mouth-filling, liqueur-like quality, without the sweetness of a liqueur.

Since the whiskies for these rarities are laid down a quarter of a century before bottling, there may be minor variations year to year. But connoisseurs of the genre look for and cherish the subtle differences between bottlings, just as enophiles compare differences in vintages of champagne or burgundy.

Ultra-premiums are often packaged in artful ceramic or crystal decanters, particularly during the holidays, which makes them alluring, exceptional gifts. However, between the costly aged malts, special decanters, and limited supply, they can be quite pricey. If you're not a true Scotch buff with a palate attuned to subtle distinctions of taste and bouquet, they may not be worth the additional cost.

ULTRA-PREMIUM SCOTCH
BUYING GUIDE

BRANDS ▶
Ballantine 30 Year (86°): Full malty, peaty complex nose. Textured, mouth-filling body, intense peat, hint of sea air; generous lacing of Islay malt. Long peaty finish; slightly sweet and woody, and a touch gruff.
Ballantine 17 Year (86°): Identically structured, but a lighter, less complex, less mature version of the 30 year old. You get what you pay for.
Chivas Royal Salute (80°): Deep, intense, complex, slightly sweet nose; full, velvety body; lots of delicate Highland malt; firm, lingering finish, by far the leader in this category.
Usquebach (86°): Whisky notes in nose; peaty, perfumey; medium-bodied; slightly sweet finish. The attractive crock bottle boasts more distinction than the whisky.
Other ultra-premiums, in extremely limited supply, are **Ambassador Twenty-Five, Bell's Royal Reserve, Grant's Own Ancient Reserve, James Martin's Fine & Rare, Johnny Walker Swing,** and **Whyte and Mackay 21 Year.**

Applications: *Bulk* Scotches are eminently mixable—ideal for cocktails, highballs, and mists. They make a light, agreeable sip poured over ice. *Premiums* may also be used in mixed drinks, but show themselves better over ice and in highballs. *Super-premiums* add an extra dimension to cocktails but, considering their rich mellow tone, are better poured over ice or with a light splash of water. *Ultra-premiums* should be sipped neat or with a splash—slowly and appreciatively.

Ireland

By definition, Irish whiskey is "a distinctive product of Ireland," made either in the Republic or in Northern Ireland. Aside from the still-incendiary question of which country first made spirits from grain, there are many parallels in the development of the whiskey industry in Ireland and Scotland. The Irish, like the Scots, vigorously resisted English taxation, and illicit distillation was rampant. The illegal whiskey was called "poteen," probably because it was made in small pot stills—easier to move if detection was imminent. The tactics that the Highland smugglers employed to evade the revenuers were also applied by Irish moonshiners, and many of the same legends of derring-do are told. To this day, a certain amount of poteen continues to be made, particularly in the west of Ireland.

However, with the reform of whiskey tax regulations in the early 1820s, licensed distilleries began to flourish, and by the late 19th century, the Irish whiskey industry had entered a period of great prosperity. During those years, in fact, Ireland was the world's leading exporter of spirits. Even in England, a request for whiskey was routinely filled with Irish, not Scotch.

In the 20th century, however, the picture changed. The lighter blended Scotch whiskies supplanted Irish in the British market, while exports to the United States were wiped out by Prohibition. The number of distilleries began to decrease, until by 1966 only four remained in the Republic of Ireland. In that year, the survivors—John Power, Tullamore Dew, John Jameson, and Cork distillery—combined to form the Irish Distillers Group, eventually consolidating all of their production in a new complex of distilleries at Midleton, Cork. In 1974, old Bushmills Distillery in Northern Ireland became part of the Group, but continues to use its own facilities. Bushmills, incidentally, claims to have the world's oldest licensed distillery—founded in 1608.

How Whiskey Is Made

Because of Ireland's association with potatoes, a persistent canard alleges that the spud is the basis of Irish whiskey. This is totally unfounded. The majority of Irish whiskeys have always been distilled primarily from barley, and originally from malted barley. But in the 19th century, Irish distillers countered a special tax on malted grain by incorporating a portion of *unmalted* barley in the mash. They decided they liked the results well enough to retain the mixture of malted and unmalted barley after the malt tax was repealed. The malt is dried in kilns, *shielded from the smoke,* so that there is no peaty taste, as in Scotch.

Although at one time Irish whiskeys were triple distilled in a series of three different pot stills, they now go through pot stills *and* continuous stills. The huge distilling complex at Midleton allows the two types of stills to be positioned beside each other. The purpose of using both is to make a full spectrum of whiskey types with different levels of proof and flavor intensity. The distillers refer to these as *"flavoring* whiskeys." They also make a certain amount of neutral, high-proof grain whiskey—mainly from corn—in continuous stills.

Aging takes place in seasoned oak barrels, some previously used for sherry. A minimum of three years in wood is required, but in practice, flavoring whiskeys are given 5 to 8 years. Before bottling, the flavoring whiskeys are mixed with a proportion of grain whiskey and left to marry for several weeks. The Irish prefer to call this process *vatting* rather than blending.

INSIDER'S GUIDE TO IRISH WHISKEY

The upheavals in the Irish whiskey industry have left their mark on production, and for a number of years, the whiskeys have been in transition. Irish distillers, like their Scottish cousins, flatly refuse to disclose the amount of low-key grain whiskeys in their final blends; but the overall trend has been to lightness of body and flavor. There is no question that today's examples are definitely less robust and pungent than those of former times, and certainly not as distinctive, one to the other. Old-time Irish whiskey drinkers correctly assert, "They ain't what they used to be." To which some reply, "And a good thing, too." Irish whiskeys are now made to be smooth, ranging from light- to medium-full, with a clean, delicate flavor.

Each of the brands produced at Midleton, and at Bushmill's in Northern Ireland, is a unique combination of flavoring whiskeys to grain whiskey, although the proportions may be altered a bit, depending on whether the whiskey is intended for the home market or for export. A small amount of pot still whiskey is also bottled.

IRISH WHISKEY BUYING GUIDE

BRANDS ▶

Most are bulk-shipped and bottled at destination. The exceptions are Paddy and Old Bushmills, which are bottled in Ireland: those listed below are all 80° except Old Bushmills' Black Bush.

Dunphy's: Lightest of the entire Irish group.

John Jameson: Fairly light, but with discernible Irish whiskey character; slight sweet perception; finishes clean and dry.

Murphy's: Clean and light.

Old Bushmills: Medium-light body, dry, malty-barley notes; closest to Scotch of all Irish whiskeys, reflecting its geographic position.

Old Bushmills Black Bush (86°): Deluxe version of Bushmills; older, fuller, velvety; winey notes; sweetness in finish; lots of pot still whiskey and a minimum of grain whiskey.

Paddy: Fairly intense flavor, some gruffness, but not unpleasant.

Powers: Retains much of the traditional Irish whiskey character; full body, distinctive barley malt impact, alcohol warmness; high proportion of pot still whiskey in the blend.

The Irish still produce some big, all pot-still whiskeys like the Jameson 12-year and 15-year old. They are not exported to the U.S. at present.

Application: The most famous Irish whiskey drink is Irish Coffee. However, Irish is still at its best with a light splash of water, or on the rocks—despite its recent turn to lightness. The lighter Irish whiskeys can also be used in standard whiskey drinks—Manhattan, Highball, Sour, Old Fashioned, etc.

The United States

Serious whiskey making in the American colonies began in the early 1700s. Emigrants from Ireland and Scotland who settled in Pennsylvania and Maryland did as they had done at home—ran small stills in which they converted part of their grain into whiskey. The popularity of this farm-grown whiskey, made mostly from rye and barley, became firmly established during the Revolution when the British blockade cut off supplies of rum, then the favorite tipple of the colonies. With the westward movement into Kentucky, pioneers discovered that they had a superb setting for whiskey production—fertile land for growing grain, ample supplies of clear water, and forests of white oak for cooperage. Since corn was the principal grain crop in these new settlements, it became the base of the whiskey that was made there.

The early history of U.S. whiskeys, like that of Scotland and Ireland, is bound up with the government's attempt to tax and regulate, on the one hand, and with the resistance of distillers on the other. One of the fledgling nation's first taxes, imposed in 1791, was an excise on whiskey. After three years of non-compliance from farmer-distillers, Alexander Hamilton, Secretary of the Treasury, sent U.S. marshals to enforce the law. The enraged whiskey makers of western Pennsylvania not only refused to pay up, but tarred and feathered the "revenuers," riding them out of town on rails. President Washington ordered out the militia to suppress the uprising, which went down in history as the Whiskey Rebellion. Many of the rebellious farmers fled over the Wilderness Road to Kentucky, supplying skilled labor for the burgeoning whiskey industry and making tax collection more difficult. Nevertheless, the incident served a major political function, establishing the rights of the new federal government to enforce its laws within the states, an important step in creating a strong central government in the U.S.

HOW U.S. WHISKEYS ARE MADE

U.S. whiskeys are a diverse lot, essentially classified by the variety of grain or grains in the mash, the proof at which they run off the still, and the length and manner of aging. Virtually no U.S. whiskey is now made in pot stills.

The U.S. government sets the following standards for *all* whiskeys:

- They must be made from a fermented mash of grain, distilled at less than 190°, and possess the taste, aroma, and characteristics generally attributed to whiskey.

- They must be reduced to no more than 125° before aging in oak containers (except corn whiskey, which need not be aged in wood), and bottled at no less than 80°.

After these basic requirements are met, U.S. whiskeys fall into three broad classifications, each with sub-groups:

- Straight Whiskeys
- Light Whiskeys
- Blended Whiskeys

Straight Whiskeys

BOURBON is the predominant example of a U.S. straight, or unblended, whiskey. It is named for Bourbon County, Kentucky, one of several places in the state where that spirit-type allegedly originated late in the 18th century. Oddly enough, the Reverend Elijah Craig of *Scott* County is most often credited with first making a bourbon-like whiskey. Actually, he was only one of many early Kentuckians who distilled whiskey from a mash of corn mixed with other grains.

Most sources attribute such bourbon innovations as the "sour mash" process and aging in charred oak kegs to Dr. James Crow, a graduate of Edinburgh University, who was appointed manager of a Kentucky distillery about 1825. He was known for the introduction of scientific methods and quality controls to fermentation, distillation, and aging, and his procedures set the standard for the new liquor. Incidentally, the name "bourbon" for such whiskey was not in popular use until after the Civil War, and it was not until 1964 that the U.S. Congress officially designated bourbon whiskey a distinctive product of the U.S.

HOW BOURBON IS MADE

The mash for bourbon must contain at least 51% corn. The *sour mash* process, associated with bourbon, has acquired a mystique in some quarters. Contrary to general impressions, sour mash does not influence the character of the distillate. It merely refers to a technique of fermentation by which part of the previous fermentation is added to the next batch of mash as a "starter" to get it going—similar to the procedure for making sourdough bread. Despite the name, it does not impart a sour or tart taste to the whiskey. The process appeals to distillers because it makes for consistency from batch to batch. But it is considered so trivial by distillers that many who follow the sour mash method do not so indicate on the label. Alternatively, *sweet mash* fermentation means that only fresh yeasts are used; no residue of a previous fermentation is added to the mash.

Bourbon, like all whiskeys first produced prior to the mid-19th century, was originally made in pot stills. It is now distilled almost entirely in continuous stills and, in accordance with government regulations for straight whiskey, it must run off at no higher than 160° and must be aged in new charred oak barrels. There are lots of legends about how charred barrels for aging made their way into distilleries. One version has it that a parsimonious whiskey maker bought up a load of kegs that had previously been used for storing fish, and then burnt the insides to get rid of the odor. The discovery, no matter how made, was felicitous, since the char inside the barrel obviously had a smoothing, mellowing effect on the raw distillate. Over a period of time it became evident that new barrels contributed more to the taste of whiskey than older ones did, so new cooperage eventually became mandatory. Although government regulations require two years of wood aging for straight whiskeys, in practice most bourbons are given at least four years. U.S. government regulations, incidentally, require that any whiskey—imported or domestic—bottled with *less* than four years in wood must indicate its age somewhere on the label. So the *absence* of an age statement tells you that the whiskey is at least four years old.

TALKING BOURBON

No Scotsman or Frenchman has gone into higher realms of lyrical rhetoric than have some Americans on the delights of their native beverage—bourbon whiskey.

One writer, discussing the excellence of bourbon as attributable to Kentucky's limestone-mountain springs, described the water as "leaping from rock to rock, laughing in its wild career until it found its haven of rest in the bosom of a mash tub—to come forth as pure nectar in the shape of bourbon."

Another said, "I give you then bourbon, the great spirit of America, worthy companion in their hours of leisure of a nation of honorable men and gracious women."

Bernard De Voto, a westerner by birth but a New Englander by choice, said of bourbon: "It wakes delight with a rich and magical plenitude of overtones and rhymes and resolves assonances and a contrapuntal succession of fleeting aftertastes."

Bottled in Bond

The designation **bottled-in-bond** indicates that the bourbon is the product of a single distillery and was distilled during a single season, kept in wood for at least four years, stored in a government supervised or "bonded" warehouse, and bottled at 100°. This procedure has no relation to quality; it merely permits distillers to postpone paying excise taxes on the whiskey until it has been bottled.

Once an important category, bonds are now an endangered species, basically because of changing tastes. A bonded bourbon, though a bit more intense, will show a familial resemblance to a lower proof bourbon bearing the same label. **J.W. Dant** and **Old Heaven Hill,** a bluegrass country favorite, have long been touted as "finds," but this is essentially based on price—that is, proof per penny.

INSIDER'S GUIDE TO BOURBON

Bourbon producers, like other distillers, have benefited from technological advances, and today's bourbons are cleaner, lighter, and smoother than they once were. Nevertheless, the distillation proof for bourbon is low enough to retain congeners, and the special manner of barrel aging adds flavor elements as well. Bourbon is a full-bodied, full-flavored whiskey, with a touch of fruit in its bouquet. The taste reflects the sweetness of corn, with a hint of vanilla from the oak and a kind of butterscotch note from the charring. There are, of course, gradations in depth of flavor and body among brands.

As with other whiskeys, many bourbons are now being bottled at 80°, and this is largely a matter of economics. Since the tax on alcohol is a big part of the cost of any spirit, reducing the proof can mean reducing the price. When inflationary increases in production costs dictate a rise in price, distillers can sometimes hold the line on a particular brand by reducing its proof from 86° to 80°. Despite distillers' disclaimers, however, it is our perception that bourbons bottled at 80° are from lighter, younger stocks, while older, richer, fuller examples come in at 86° and higher. In fact, there is a small but significant category of fine bourbons bottled at between 101° and 114°. These bourbons have the age and character to balance the additional alcohol, and are sought by aficionados.

Before proof statements were required on labels, bourbon fanciers would shake the bottle to watch the bubbles rise and break. The higher the proof (up to 100°) the longer the bubble or "bead" would hold. This presumably reflected the fullness, almost oiliness, of the body. Another way of checking this was to note the way the whiskey clung to the sides of the glass when it was swirled a bit. Such tests are no longer necessary to determine proof, but you can get a clue to the fullness of the bourbon by the length of time the aroma remains in an emptied glass; an hour or longer at room temperature indicates a full-bodied bourbon.

 BOURBON BUYING GUIDE

BRANDS ▶

Ancient Age (86°): Hints of spice; medium range in nose and mouth; smooth, clean.

Benchmark (86°): Hints of vanilla and spice; fairly smooth; medium body, balanced; lingers on the palate.

Early Times (80°): Medium-light body; fruit in aroma; easy to drink.

Henry McKenna (80°): Light, fragrant nose; medium-light, soft body; nutty, complex; slightly sweet finish; well-structured.

Hiram Walker Ten High (80°): Slightly acrid, woody nose; the barrel overpowers the whiskey.

Jim Beam (80°): Lightish body; sweet perception in mouth; tastes young.

Maker's Mark (90°): Rich, brandy-like nose with hints of vanilla; dry, fairly smooth; substantial but not heavy; bourbon the way old-timers remember it. *Note:* Until recently this was a small, family-owned distillery. It is now a Hiram Walker property, and production is expanding. The new proprietors claim they will maintain the quality. We hope they do.

Old Crow (80°): Inadequate bouquet; some vanilla but rather flat; medium-full body.

Old Grand-Dad (86°): Fairly aromatic; hints of vanilla and fruit; moderately full, smooth; butterscotch notes.

The brands detailed below have one element in common: They are all high-proof.

Eagle Rare (101°): Full nose and body; vanilla and fruit aromas; nutty, deep taste; clean, smooth, mature.

Ezra Brooks (101°): Vanilla and caramel notes; medium-full body; clean, balanced.

Grand-Dad Barrel Proof (114°): Bottled straight from the barrel, hence the name; rich, full, sweetish vanilla nose; full, round body, mouth-filling; definite sweet perceptions in taste and finish.

Old Weller (107°): Flowery bouquet, medium-full; sweet, perfumey; not enough body to cover the alcohol; pleasing finish.

Wild Turkey (101°): Lacks flavor intensity, despite the generous proof; fairly sweet, smooth; some off odors.

Application: Bourbon and branch (a Southern term for spring water) is preferred in the areas where bourbon is made, and where the fullest bourbons are the most appreciated. Bourbon is also served on the rocks or mixed in standard whiskey drinks—and, of course, in Mint Juleps.

One of the few Straight Rye whiskeys now being distilled in the U.S. The term "rye" is often applied—inaccurately—to blended whiskeys.

INSIDER'S GUIDE TO
OTHER STRAIGHT WHISKEYS

TENNESSEE WHISKEY is, obviously, produced in Tennessee. It is *not* a bourbon, although it is quite similar in process and style. Made like a sour mash bourbon, Tennessee has one extra step—the spirit is filtered through charcoal immediately after distillation. Much is made of this point.

 ## TENNESSEE WHISKEY
BUYING GUIDE

BRANDS ▶

Jack Daniel's Old No. 7 Black Label (90°): The flagship brand; not only the leading Tennessee whiskey, but outsells most bourbons; fairly light and smooth in the mouth, with a slight sweet edge; sharp, acrid notes in the aroma; the aftertaste a bit dirty and woody. Allegedly favored by entertainers and personalities, we feel it is over-rated; apparently the company's advertising proficiency exceeds its distilling technique.

Jack Daniel's Green Label: A younger, lighter, less expensive version of Black Label.

George Dickel Old #12 (90°): The only other Tennessee whiskey in general distribution and a distant second in sales to Jack Daniel's Black; fuller and a bit dryer than Daniel's—more in the old-time whiskey style; at its best with "branch" or over rocks. Note that "Old #12" does not mean it is twelve years old.

George Dickel Old #8: The opposite number to Jack Daniel's Green Label.

Lem Motlow: Made by Daniel's distillery; every drop proudly guaranteed to be *less* than one year old. Aside from being rough, it's not bad; available only in Tennessee.

RYE WHISKEY must be made with 51% rye grain. Distillation proof, cooperage, and aging requirements are the same as for bourbon. Rye is a full-bodied, pungent spirit, with a noticeable whiskey taste. Though popular at one time, very little is produced these days. But the term "rye" lives on—mistakenly used as a generic name for blended whiskeys, particularly in the northeastern part of the U.S. Most people who casually ask for rye when they mean blended whiskey would be quite startled at the tangy taste of true rye whiskey.

BRANDS ▶

Just about the only rye brands available are the rather gruff **Old Overholt** (86°), affectionately referred to as "Old Overalls," and **Wild Turkey** (101°), a name ordinarily associated with bourbon. "Turkey," aged eight years, is relatively mellow and balanced despite its high proof, with a pleasant, spicy aroma.

STRAIGHT WHISKEY is made like straight bourbon or straight rye, but from a mixture of grains, none of which accounts for 51% of the mash. Not too much is around.

BRANDS ▶
Michter's Pot Still Sour Mash Straight Whiskey:
Michter's product deserves mention, since it dates back to 1753, and the distillery has been designated a National Historic Landmark. Michter's bottles two versions, an 86° and a 101°, both six years old and smooth, with pleasant whiskey taste, although the 101° is a bit harsher and fuller in taste than the 86° version.

CORN WHISKEY, to qualify as a straight, must be made with at least 80% corn, distilled at less than 160°, and aged for a minimum of two years in new or used *uncharred* barrels. It's considerably lighter and quite a bit harsher than bourbon. A fair amount of corn whiskey is bottled at less than two years. Most is consumed in the South, where it's made; a few novelty packages are available, such as the mason jar of Georgia Moon "less than 30 days old." The chances are that the jar adds more to production costs than the contents.

The U.S. government's standards of identity for straight whiskeys also mention **MALT WHISKEY** (made with malted barley), **WHEAT WHISKEY,** and **MALTED RYE WHISKEY.** If any of these are now made, they are strictly local phenomena.

Light Whiskey

Light whiskey is a relatively new type of American whiskey, having been officially declared a category on July 1, 1972. The lightness in "Light" is intrinsic, deriving from the way the whiskey is elaborated. Any type, or proportion, of grains may be used, but most distillers prefer a high percentage of corn. Light whiskey runs off the still at high proofs—between 161° and 189° and thus has fewer congeners than do other U.S. whiskeys. The distillate is aged in *previously used* or *uncharred new* cooperage. This, too, accounts for the lighter body and subdued taste, since the wood contributes few flavor elements during aging.

When Light whiskey was first launched, the American distilling industry had high hopes for its success as a separate category, especially as an alternative to the imported light Scotch and Canadian whiskies. But the interest never developed, and while Light whiskey is still made, it is used mainly as a component for blended whiskey. Nevertheless, there is a consumer need for such a product, and Light whiskey may some day be revived.

BRANDS ▶
A few Light whiskey brands are still on the market: **Barton QT Premium, Jacquin Light,** and **Park & Tilford American Light.** None is particularly distinctive.

Blended Whiskey

The basic requirement for any U.S. blended whiskey is that it contain at least 20% straight whiskey at 100°; the remainder may be unaged grain neutral spirits. The category became important as a result of World War II, when it was seized on by U.S. distillers as a valid way to stretch the dwindling wartime supply of aged straight whiskey. Some of the early efforts were downright awful, but by the middle 1940s, the industry had the problem largely in hand, and managed to turn out blends that were balanced and consistent.

This restrained new liquor coincided with the turn toward lighter flavor, and for the next two decades or so, it became the most popular spirit type in the U.S. Nevertheless, blends lacked a clear identity. By-passing the term "blended whiskey," people would simply request a particular brand, or they would refer to the whiskey as "rye" in the eastern part of the U.S. and as "bourbon" in the west—obvious cases of mistaken identity.

Though still a major category, blended whiskey has been losing favor since the 1960s. It is perceived as too bland by Scotch and bourbon fanciers and as too robust by those attracted to the low-key Canadian whiskies and vodka. It is now overshadowed by all these spirits.

For a while, some distillers hoped that blended whiskey could be given more appeal if Light whiskey replaced the neutral grain spirits. They reasoned that when straight whiskeys are mixed with Light whiskeys, the blend has a structure similar to blended Scotch in that it is a mixture of *whiskeys*. This approach did not take hold, and now only a few brands are made this way. The rest have moved back to mixtures of straight whiskey and neutral spirits or, in some cases, to straight whiskey with neutral spirits and Light whiskey.

INSIDER'S GUIDE TO BLENDED WHISKEY

Blended whiskey tastes like whiskey—but without any single distinctive characteristic. It's probably closest to bourbon, but lacks bourbon's greater intensity of flavor and fuller body. In many ways, blends are a confusing group. Brand name has always been emphasized over category, and there is, in fact, no one term that identifies a spirit as blended whiskey. Some brands call themselves "American Whiskey—A Blend;" others "American Blended Whiskey;" still others, just plain "Blended Whiskey." Nevertheless, the label offers a savvy consumer some information. If the blend contains grain spirits, the exact percentage *must* be shown; it usually appears in small print on a neck or back label. If *nothing* about components appears on the labels, the contents of the bottle are *all* whiskey—a mixture of at least 20% straight, with the rest Light—and percentages need not be revealed. The straight whiskey in a blend is the informing flavor and source of character.

BRANDS ▶
All are 80° unless noted otherwise.

Seagram 7 Crown and **Calvert Extra:** both are *all* whiskey, revealing this in their balanced smoothness and depth of flavor; Seagram 7 is the lighter-bodied of the two.

Schenley: 35% straight whiskey and 65% grain neutral spirits; not as smooth as Seagram or Calvert, but fairly full-flavored.

Fleischmann Preferred (90° in the east), **Kessler,** and **Imperial** are all 72½% grain spirits; the latter two are quite light, almost thin; Fleischmann's is fuller and a bit harsh.

Application: Blended whiskeys are suitable for use in all mixed whiskey drinks. Fuller examples can be served over ice or with a splash of soda or water.

Canada

Canada's whisky industry, like that of the United States, began with its grain farmers, who did a little distilling on the side. And, as in the U.S., professional distillers had largely taken over the production of whisky by the beginning of the 20th century. At that time, Canadian's present style developed—light, clean, and muted in flavor. Distillers turned to corn, barley, wheat, and other grains that yielded a less pungent spirit than rye, originally the predominant grain used for Canadian whisky. However, Canadians never got over the habit of referring to their native whisky as "rye," although the name is no longer accurate.

How Canadian Whisky Is Made

The Canadian government, which closely regulates its whisky industry, does *not* set requirements for the proportion of grains to be used, distilling proofs, or type of cooperage for aging. Distillers have considerable latitude in developing their own styles. All, however, use the continuous still to produce a light-bodied whisky, free of aggressive flavor notes. For the most part, aging takes place in used barrels. Canadian whiskies may be bottled after three years of aging, but in practice most get from four to six.

Individuality in Canadian whisky is a function of blending—combining whiskies made from different grains, aged for varying periods until just the right balance is achieved. The late Samuel Bronfman, founder of the Seagram Company, characterized blending as "the art of successfully combining...in such a manner that the whole is better than the sum of its parts."

INSIDER'S GUIDE TO CANADIAN WHISKY

There are two main Canadian whisky types: **bulk** and **bottled in Canada.**

Bulk Canadians are shipped in barrels and bottled at their destination, and they comprise the majority of Canadian whiskies sold in the United States today. Most are four years old, and are usually bottled at 80°. Not surprisingly, they are the least expensive Canadian whiskies. The bulks are blended to be particularly light and mixable. They offer the taste of whisky but not the aftertaste; individual brands are not notably distinctive.

BRANDS ▶
Black Velvet (80°): Exceedinglly light; is this side of vodka.
Canadian Mist (80°): Light, with a slightly harsh note, explained perhaps by a line of very fine print on the back label which reads, "This whisky is thirty-six months old."

Lord Calvert (80°): Clean, light-medium in body; a suggestion of nuttiness.

Windsor Supreme (80°): A bit fuller; sweet, chemical taste.

Bottled in Canada Canadians include older whiskies in their blends and, with one or two exceptions, are bottled at 86.8°. They have rounder flavor and body than the bulks. As a group, bottled-in-Canada whiskies are now outdistanced by the less expensive bulks, but two individual brands—**Seagram's V.O.** and **Canadian Club**—still rank among the five most popular liquors in the U.S. Careful shoppers should take note that the Canadian tax stamp strip over the bottle cap has a particular year printed on it. According to the Canadian government, this is the birth date of the *youngest* whisky in the blend.

BRANDS ▶

Canadian Club (86.8°): A bit lighter than V.O.; not as clean.

Crown Royal (80°): Much more aroma and body than other Canadians; surprisingly full and round.

Schenley O.F.C. (86.8°): More taste of grain than V.O.; smooth and round in mouth, but woody.

Seagram V.O. (86.8°): Very light whisky aroma and taste; smooth, clean, undistinctive.

Application: Use Canadians like other whiskies—lighter types in mixed drinks, fuller ones on the rocks or in highballs.

Japan

The Japanese have been making whisky for more than half a century, and Suntory—the largest distiller—is one of the top five liquor companies in the world. Suntory describes its product as "slightly east of Scotch," a neat phrase and probably more accurate than most advertising lingo, since a number of Japanese whiskies are laced with a measure of malt whisky, imported from Scotland.

Most Japanese whisky, like Scotch, is a blend that includes a modest amount of pot still malt whisky and a larger quantity of column still whisky made from a mixture of grains. The malt whisky comes off the still at about 130°, the grain whisky in the range of 180°, and both are aged in oak casks for varying lengths of time, depending on the style of the intended blend. One can detect a hint of smokiness in the flavor of Japanese whiskies, especially the more expensive examples. But on the whole, they are medium-bodied, balanced, and delicate in taste.

BRANDS ▶

Suntory is the only Japanese distillery significant in the export market. It currently sends four of its many labels to the U.S. In ascending order of price and Scotch-like character, they are **Suntory Royal, Suntory Old, Suntory Reserve,** and **Suntory Signature** (packaged in a crystal decanter).

Nikka, the other major distiller, and **Kirin-Seagram,** a recent venture, do not at present export their whiskies to the west to any extent.

Applications: Japanese whiskies can be used in the same way as blended Scotch whiskies.

GLOSSARY

BEER: The liquid resulting from the fermentation of the *wort* (see below). It contains between 5% and 10% alcohol. Also called "distiller's beer" or "wash."

GRAIN NEUTRAL SPIRITS: Spirits distilled from grain at or above 190°.

MALT: Germinated or sprouted grain, usually barley. As the grain sprouts, it develops enzymes capable of converting starch into maltose (hence the name "malt") and other sugars.

MASH: A mixture of coarsely ground, dried grain and hot water, which is the raw material for fermentation. It always contains a percentage of *malt* (see above) that converts the starch into fermentable sugar.

WASH: See *beer.*

WORT: A sweet liquid drawn from the mash, which is fermented with yeasts.

Brandy

BRANDY is a spirit made by fermenting and distilling fruit. When made from a fruit *other than* grapes, the word "Brandy" is linked with the name of that fruit. When the label reads "Brandy" alone—without any qualifying description—it *must* be derived from grape wine. Brandy, in fact, has been characterized as the "soul of wine."

Brandy is made in just about every wine-producing region of the world and displays enormous diversity. Generally speaking, all brandies exhibit a certain fruitiness in aroma and taste, but can range from clean, soft, and light-bodied to intense, pruney, and richly full-bodied.

The story of brandy's beginnings is virtually the early history of of the distillation of potable spirits. Wine was the raw material for the *aqua vitae* or *eau de vie* described by 12th- and 13th-century chroniclers of the distillation process. Knowledge and practice of distillation spread through the wine-making regions of southern Europe in succeeding centuries. The Dutch traders who introduced the spirit to northern Europe called it *brandewijn*—burnt wine; this was subsequently shortened to "brandy."

Brandies of France

Regardless of where brandy was originally distilled, France was the first country to produce it for widespread commercial sale. Brandy is made all over France, but the country is particularly noted for two examples—cognac, the most renowned brandy in the world, and armagnac, its oldest brandy. To this day, they remain the benchmark for all brandies, no matter where produced.

Cognac

By now it is a cliché: All cognac is brandy, but not all brandy is cognac. In fact, the only brandy in the world that may legally be labeled "cognac," comes from the Charente and Charente-Maritime departments in west-central France, comprising roughly 250,000 acres. The town of Cognac sits squarely in the center and lends its name to the celebrated brandy of the region. The geographical limits of the relatively small area in which cognac can be made were set by the French government in 1909. No other place in the world may use the word on its brandy products. And on the rare occasion when the name has been misappropriated, France has made it an international issue.

The cognac region was known for its wines as early as the Middle Ages. But by the beginning of the 17th century, these were so heavily taxed that *vignerons* were forced to charge prohibitive prices. Even more to the point, foreign customers complained that the wines were deteriorating during the voyage from France and becoming undrinkable. French winemakers turned to distilling their wines as an answer to both problems. Traders enthusiastically embraced the new distilled product, undoubtedly recognizing a fertile market for it in their own countries and in the cold lands of northern Europe.

As demand for the brandy of the region grew, professional distillers began to take over from the small growers, followed by *négociants*—shippers—who assumed responsibility for the blending and aging operations. In fact, many of today's leading cognac houses started just this way during the 18th and early 19th centuries. Several who founded firms that still flourish were emigrants from the British Isles. Among them were Jean Martell, who came from the Isle of Jersey in 1715; Richard Hennessey,

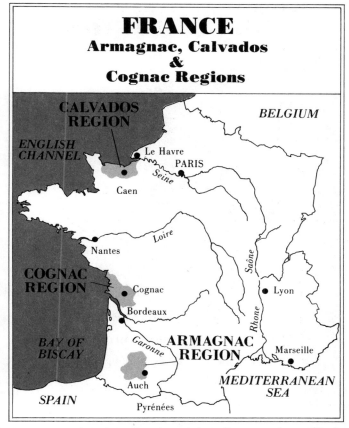

FRANCE
Armagnac, Calvados
&
Cognac Regions

An overview of the finest brandies made in France, and arguably, in the world. They are all distinctive—offering different satisfactions.

from Ireland in 1765; and Thomas Hine, from England at the end of the 18th century—all helped build the acceptance of "brandy from Cognac" in Britain, and around the world. Today, more than 80% of cognac sales are outside of France. The U.S. has recently displaced the U.K. as the premier export market, but Hong Kong boasts the largest per capita consumption.

HOW COGNAC IS MADE
The growing area of the cognac region is subdivided into six zones, based mainly on soil and climatic conditions. The most highly regarded are the *Grande Champagne* and *Petite Champagne* districts. This use of *Champagne,* incidentally, has nothing to do with France's celebrated sparkling wine; it comes from the word *champ,* meaning field.

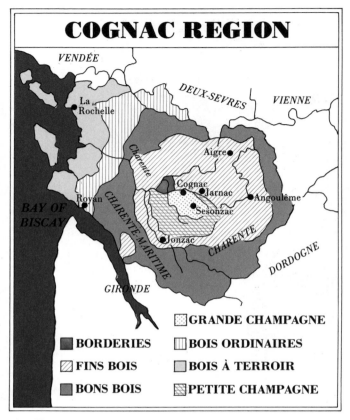

COGNAC REGION

GRANDE CHAMPAGNE

BORDERIES

BOIS ORDINAIRES

FINS BOIS

BOIS À TERROIR

BONS BOIS

PETITE CHAMPAGNE

An old map of the Cognac region showing the various geographic zones. Although seven zones are indicated here there are only six today—the Bois à Terroir, having been combined with the Bois Ordinaires, now takes the latter designation.

Ten or so different white grapes can legally be used for cognac, but the Ugni Blanc, also known as the St. Emilion, is the major variety.

The wines of Cognac are thin, low in alcohol, and acidic—scarcely drinkable. Paradoxically, these peevish qualities make for richer brandy. In fact, everything is geared to heightening the organoleptic impact of the final product. The wine is not filtered before distillation, lest some of the minute, flavor-giving particles be lost. French law dictates that distillation must be completed by March 31, while the wine is in its bloom of youth—fruity and unoxidized. Also pertinent is the stubborn adherence to the alembic or pot still. This ancient, somewhat inefficient device yields a low-proof spirit that retains a high percentage of the essential flavor components, thus providing the potential for a more aromatic and complex brandy than the higher proof distillates that run off column stills.

Cognac goes through two distillations. The first, called the *brouillis,* results in a rank, murky spirit with approximately 28% alcohol content. The heart of the second distillation (the heads and tales are set aside to be redistilled) is called *la bonne chauffe.* It emerges from the still at about 140° and, like all newly made spirits, is colorless and raw. It acquires smoothness, finesse, and color as it ages in wood. Oak casks are mandatory. At one time, all the wood came from the nearby forests of Limousin, but as Limousin lumber becomes scarcer, it is being supplemented with oak from Tronçais.

The age of the cask contributes to the style of cognac desired; new oak imparts more taste to the spirit than does aged wood. A young cognac usually spends some time in new cooperage but within a year it is transferred to older barrels. Lesser grades of cognac, which are to be bottled fairly young, are given more time in new wood so that flavor develops quickly. In fact, it is not unknown for oak chips, *le boisé,* to be added to the barrel to hasten the effect of the wood. On the other hand, the more promising distillates are soon moved into seasoned oak to mature more slowly. Firms marketing the lighter, more delicate, and softer cognacs almost always do their aging in used barrels.

As cognac ages, a substantial 3% to 5% evaporates through the pores of the oak barrels. This emission, locally referred to as the "angels' share," scents the atmosphere in the town of Cognac and its environs, and nourishes a black fungus that covers the walls and roofs of cognac warehouses. However, it can be said that the angels pay for their drink: As the spirits mature, they mellow, taking on bouquet, body, subtlety, and savor.

Although a new batch of cognac is distilled every year, there is no vintage cognac bottled today. The cognac on the market is a blend of different years and usually different growing districts.

The virtuosos of cognac are the master blenders, and their skills—passed from generation to generation—may be the most important ingredient in a bottle. The major cognac houses maintain huge inventories from different zones, vineyards, and years, including vintages well over a century old. These rarities are stored in glass demijohns, not in oak, to prevent further evaporation and excessive woodiness. It is the master's job to fashion this kaleidoscope of flavors and aromas into a harmonious blend.

INSIDER'S GUIDE TO COGNAC

Cognac will naturally vary according to blend, age, and style, but can be generally described as fragrant and mellow. One's first awareness of cognac—any cognac—is of the heady aroma. No other spirit presents the intense, complex, suffusing bouquet and staying power that cognac offers. The aroma lingers in the emptied glass, and the better the cognac, the longer it will remain.

Since cognacs are blends, no age may be stated on the label, but cognac regulations do provide a system for establishing the age of any given barrel of cognac. Its official birth date is April 1 following the harvest of the previous fall, and it becomes a year older every April 1 thereafter, until its sixth birthday. Records beyond that point have no *legal* status. Of course every cognac house maintains its own inventory records and presumably knows the precise age and source of all its stocks.

The jumble of stars and cryptic initials on cognac labels are an accumulation of history, tradition, and crude merchandising. The first heavenly symbol appeared sometime in the 19th century, after a bountiful harvest during which a comet streaked across the heavens. A star was placed on the label to commemorate both events. Next year's harvest was equally good, so another star was added. After that, galactic adornments proliferated, with labels looking more and more like astrological charts.

Then came the letters—a tribute to Great Britain's importance in the cognac market, since they stand for English words. VSOP, for instance, is *V*ery *S*uperior *O*ld *P*ale. "Pale" does not mean anything now, but originally it was intended to suggest that the cognac was natural rather than darkened or flavored with additives. In VS*E*P, the "E" stands for "Extra," while XO is short for "extrordinary" or "extraordinarily old." Locals of the cognac region have their own droll interpretation of some of these designations, insisting that VSOP is *Versez Sans Oublier Personne*—pour without omitting anyone. A noble sentiment.

Reading a Cognac Label

The cognac industry eventually settled on the following general guidelines in their use of stars, letters, or names on labels.
- Three stars or the letters VS or VSP indicate that the minimum

THE BLENDER'S ART

If a TV camera were smuggled into a master blender's quarters, it would show him swirling brandy in a blue 4-ounce tulip-shaped glass, barely one-third full. Swirling liberates the bouquet, blue glass masks the color of the sample so it can not affect perceptions, and it is easier to warm cognac—and thus release more vapors—in a small glass that fits comfortably in the hand. The blender then thrusts his nose into the glass and inhales searchingly. His keen proboscis will pick up any off-flavor, in which event the entire lot is discarded. Another quick sniff grades and positions the brandy, and a few drops on the tongue confirm the olfactory judgment. Swallowing is considered bad form. After the brandy is expelled, the finish, or aftertaste, is noted. Is it harsh or bitter? Balanced? Does it break up quickly or linger persistently on the palate, filling the mouth with waves of intriguing flavors? After forming his opinions of the various lots, the master prepares his *cuvée* or blend—selecting this sample for aroma, that one for finesse or elegance, yet another for body—like a weaver choosing strands for a tapestry. And, like an exquisite tapestry, the finished blend will be a complete, integrated work of art.

When ready for bottling, the cognac is reduced to the desired proof—80° as a rule—and the color may be rectified with a bit of caramel.

age for the youngest cognac in the blend is 2 years. In practice, the average age is 3 to 5 years.

- The letters VSOP, VSEP, VSO, and VO indicate a minimum age of 4 years for the youngest cognac, with an average age of between 10 and 15 years.
- Cognacs labeled with special names—*Napoleon, Cordon Bleu, Triomphe, Vieille Réserve, XO, Extra Anniversaire,* etc.—have a minimum age of 6 years for the youngest, but in fact run an average age of upwards of 20 years. On occasion, the words *Age Inconnu*—Age Unknown—appear on this class of bottlings. This is meant to imply that the cognac is of great age, even though no figure may be given.
- When cognac is labeled *Napoleon,* it does not mean the cognac came from Napoleon's cellar or dates back to the time of Napoleon. The name merely pays tribute to the Little Corporal's devotion to cognac—shared by his less illustrious nephew, Napoleon III. In fact, there is some question as to which of the two actually inspired the designation—except in the case of Courvoisier, which proudly asserts that Napoleon I visited Château Courvoisier and sampled the pride of the house.

- The words *Grande Champagne* or *Grande Fine Champagne* indicate that all the grapes came from the premier growing zone, the Grand Champagne. *Fine Champagne* means that the grapes were grown in the two top zones, the *Grande* and *Petite Champagne*, with more than half from the Grande Champagne.

Most cognac brands, particularly from the larger firms, are available in a range from Three Star all the way up to special limited bottlings blended from the very oldest and finest stocks. These generally commemorate some historic occasion—and their issue is invariably timed to catch the holiday season. They are always costly and, if presented in fine crystal or porcelain decanters, can be astronomically expensive. Packaging aside, price—at the very least—gives a rough indication of the category of cognac in the bottle. VSOP usually represents the best value in terms of the price/quality ratio, offering enough in bouquet and flavor to hold its own in a brandy snifter. If you have just one bottle of cognac in your bar, the logical choice is VSOP. The "Napoleon" level can be twice as expensive as VSOP, and worth the difference to aficionados who enjoy and appreciate cognac's subtleties and complexities.

★   **COGNAC**   ★
BUYING GUIDE

Unless otherwise noted, the cognacs described below are VSOP.

BRANDS ▶

Courvoisier: Appealing oaky-vanilla bouquet; rather full-bodied and round without harsh edges.

Hennessey: Delicate fragrance with hints of fruit; medium light-bodied with good balance.

Martell: Clean with grapey, spicy-oaky notes prominent in the bouquet; moderately full and mouth-filling.

Rémy-Martin: Smooth and fragrant with a silky body; light side of medium-bodied; no tannin or woody notes intrude.

The preceding cognacs are the major brands in the world market. Other well-rated cognacs include:

Bisquit: Subtle, rich bouquet; fruity and clean with smooth body; slight sweet perception in finish.

Hine: Elegant and smooth; hint of sweetness.

Also: **Camus, Dénis-Mounie, Monnet,** and **Otard.**

Delamain and **Ragnaud-Sabourin** are small houses noted for the finesse and delicacy of their cognacs. The latter's **Grand Réserve Fontvieille** is exquisite. Delamain's lowest designation, **Pale & Dry,** is older than VSOP.

There are also a number of fine old cognacs in very limited distribution that are more likely to be found in high-level French restaurants than in shops. They include **Jean Danflou Grande Champagne Extra, Madame Gaston Briand Grande Fine Champagne, Croizet Age Inconnu,** and **Frapin Château de Fontpinot.**

Application: Three Star and VSOP cognacs may be served in a snifter, over ice, in highballs, with orange juice, or in such brandy-based cocktails as the Sidecar or Stinger—they can even substitute for whisky in the Manhattan, Sour, or Old Fashioned. Older, finer cognacs are best drunk neat—and the type of glass is important. A liqueur glass is simply too small to allow room for the bouquet to develop, while an over-sized balloon-shaped snifter concentrates the fragrance so much that it can become overpowering. Ideally, the glass should be thin, permitting the warmth of the hand to pass through; it should taper towards the top to capture the bouquet; and it should have a capacity of 5 to 6 ounces, although no more than an ounce or so should be poured at one time. Cognac buffs breathe the brandy as much as drink it—swirling and sniffing—probing for the innermost depths of its perfume before finally imbibing it. In the Far East, cognac is taken with food, like wine—either straight, over ice, or mixed with water.

Armagnac

Armagnac, like cognac, was given an *appellation contrôlée* by the French government in 1909. This ensures that the name armagnac can be given only to brandy made in a delimited area in the heart of southwestern France—part of what was once the ancient province of Gascony.

Armagnac has been made for over 500 years, predating cognac by almost 2 centuries. The art of distillation came to Gascony via the Moors from across the border in Spain. Despite its earlier start, armagnac has never achieved cognac's fame. It was produced in small quantities by individual producers in a secluded inland part of the country, which made its distribution difficult. On the other hand, the Cognaçais, with easy access to the sea, were able to introduce their product all over Europe. Even now, armagnac's production is modest—less than 10% of cognac's total.

For centuries, armagnac remained a well-kept secret, known only locally and to a handful of connoisseurs outside the country. As recently as a decade ago, less than a half-dozen brands were consistently in the export market. But armagnac took a great leap forward in the early 1970s with the advent of the *nouvelle cuisine* chef-stars such as Michel Guérard (himself a Gascon) and others. Ever on the lookout for touches that would add distinctiveness to

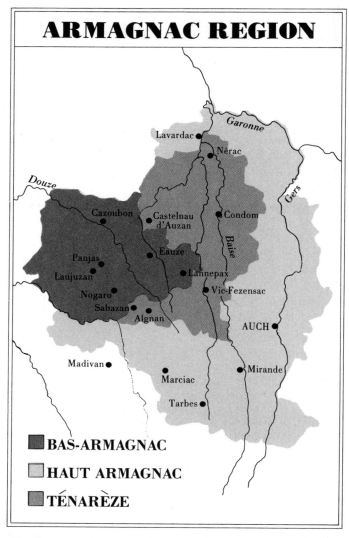

ARMAGNAC REGION

BAS-ARMAGNAC

HAUT ARMAGNAC

TÉNARÈZE

Armagnac occupies much of the old Gascony region, land of the musketeers. It has remained something of a French secret because of its remote location. Even today, travel connections are difficult.

their restaurants, they discovered that fine old *vintage* armagnacs—the unblended product of a single year—were to be found throughout the region. They seized on these rarities for their exalted hostelries, and suddenly armagnac became chic— *the* after-dinner *digestif*. From this springboard, aided and abetted by the promotional efforts of its producers, armagnac is now achieving a new recognition and popularity.

How Armagnac Is Made

Only white grapes may be used for armagnac, the principal varieties being Ugni Blanc, Colombard, and Folle Blanche. These grapes are grown in three sub-regions of the delimited armagnac area: Bas Armagnac, Ténarèze, and Haute Armagnac, but only the first two matter.

Distillation takes place in the traditional *alambic armagnaçais,* a unique variation of a continuous still—small and inefficient—nothing like the huge monsters found in modern distilleries.

The wines go through a single distillation and trickle out at about 110°, thus retaining a high proportion of aromatic flavoring elements. The new armagnac is colorless, with an assertive bouquet and flavor that demand longer aging for palatibility than is needed for cognac.

Along with other wine and spirit producers, armagnac makers are searching for ways to reduce the time required for maturation. One approach to the problem is a recent change in armagnac regulations, which now permit double distillation in pot stills. This yields a somewhat lighter, smoother brandy that, when blended with young, traditionally distilled armagnacs, makes them palatable at an earlier age. Some producers are now blending in up to 30% pot still armagnac, but only in lower-level bottlings.

At one time, all barrels for aging armagnac were made from oak grown in the local forests of Monlezun, which added its own special taste to the spirit. But supplies of the Monlezun oak have dwindled and are now being supplemented with barrels made of Limousin and Tronçais oak, the same as those used for cognac. To what extent this will affect armagnac's flavor remains to be seen.

INSIDER'S GUIDE TO ARMAGNAC

Armagnac firms have typically been small and individualistic, concerned with quality, although not necessarily with a consistent house style. That may be changing, since some of the old names are being bought up by large, marketing-oriented firms from outside the area. Despite this and other modifications

A venerable example from Bas-Armagnac, the most esteemed sub-region of the Armagnac area. After the brandy is drained a pruney fragrance remains in the glass, continuing to give pleasure.

mentioned, the Armagnacais insist they will maintain the brandy's unique character and that they have no intention of making imitation cognac. Armagnac, particularly when young, is noticeably more intense and pungent than cognac. As it ages, its forthright nature becomes rounder, mellower, and more balanced, but the spirit remains full-bodied, with a grapey, pruney, earthy quality and a noticeable hint of wood.

Armagnac uses much the same system of stars, letters, and names on labels as does cognac (see page 54) to indicate levels of age and quality, and is subject to essentially the same regulations. A minor difference is that for the "Napoleon" category of armagnac, five years is the minimum age for the youngest brandy in the blend, whereas cognac requires six years. In practice, however, armagnac of all classes—and particularly the top levels—averages much more age than the required minimums.

Determining the age of a vintage armagnac is not as simple as it would appear. Year of birth is less significant than length of wood aging, since spirits—unlike wine—neither change nor improve after bottling. Armagnac producers contend that they bottle vintages shortly before shipping, so the age is approximately the difference between the vintage date and the time the bottle becomes commercially available. However, the welter of international liquor laws does not allow for *legal* guarantees of true age. The label on a bottle of 1900-vintage armagnac exported to the U.S., for instance, may bear the words, "Aged in wood seven years." But the fact is that this unimpressive statement represents the maximum certification that the French armagnac bureau can give. In France itself, the label on a vintage armagnac may state the date of bottling, but it is only a *claim* by the producer, who bears the burden of proof if challenged.

Even the modest quantity of vintage armagnac now available, both in France and in the export market, will be diminishing, so if your heart is set on vintage armagnac, buy it now. Producers are recognizing that their old stocks are a precious, irreplaceable commodity, too valuable to expend in single bottlings. Perhaps more important, they feel that for the discerning armagnac drinker, blends are generally more rewarding, offering greater complexity and subtlety than vintages.

The glamor of vintage bottlings notwithstanding, the vast majority of armagnacs are blends of different years and usually of two of the sub-regions. If the name of a sub-region appears on the label, all the contents of the bottle came from that area. Most armagnacs shipped out of the country are VSOP, although more examples of the higher levels are becoming available.

Traditionally, armagnac was packaged in a *basquaise* bottle, a squat, flat-sided flask reminiscent of those once used by smugglers in the Pyrenees mountains. However, there is a shift to standard bottles. Proof is being lowered, too, settling out in the low 80s rather than the 86° to 90° that was once the norm.

THE TRAVELING STILL

Until fairly recently, a portable *alambic armagnacais* was a fairly common sight among the vineyards and farms of the armagnac region during the distilling season. The still was mounted on a two-wheel cart and trundled about the countryside by itinerant distillers called *bouillers de cru.* They serviced small growers who did not have their own stills, stopping at each property just long enough for the *vigneron* to turn his bit of wine into brandy. These traveling stills have now been replaced by slightly bigger, fixed models owned by either cooperatives or larger individual producers.

ARMAGNAC BUYING GUIDE

BRANDS ▶

Clés des Ducs: Fragrant and fruity; sweet edge in finish; medium-bodied.

De Montal: Woody-spicy fragrance; pruney-fruity finish; medium-full; also available in vintage bottlings.

Larressingle: Full-bodied, spicy, pruney; planning to offer vintage bottlings.

Loubère: Bas Armagnac; round, smooth, dry; wood and chocolate in the finish.

Marquis de Caussade: An old label under new management, which is blending toward the "newer" armagnac style—smooth and less assertive; also available in vintage bottlings.

Samalens: Bas Armagnac; pruney fragrance characteristic of sub-region; dry, smooth; now using some pot still armagnac in its VSOP, a clean, medium-bodied blend.

Sempé: Piney-spicy bouquet; full-bodied; sweet edge with perceptions of chocolate, spice, and prunes.

Other less available brands include:

Chabot: Full-bodied example found mainly in duty-free shops in international airports.

Domaine de Lahitte: Well-aged, particularly full and pungent Bas Armagnac.

Janneau and **J. de Malliac:** better-known in England than the U.S.; both on the light side.

Marquis de Montesquiou: Full, chocolatey, and brusque.

Hubert Dayton, Laberdolive, and **Michel Reynaud** offer superb vintage bottlings, but they are hard to find.

Application: Sip neat in a 5-ounce brandy snifter or the type of glass described in the cognac section (page 57).

Other French Brandies

Brandy is distilled in wine areas all over France, and most of it is quite ordinary. For the most part, these brandies are made in conventional continuous stills and aged a couple of years or so before bottling. They are the ones poured in French bars when customers ask for a *fine*. Some French brandy makers have adopted the stars, letters, and names ("Napoleon" is a particular favorite) seen on cognac and armagnac labels. They have absolutely no meaning on ordinary brandies, and are in fact misleading. French brandies made from fruit other than grapes are discussed further on.

California Brandy

For all practical purposes, California brandy is synonymous with U.S. brandy. None of the other forty-odd wine producing states make brandy in commercial quantities.

Brandy making came to California more than 200 years ago with the Spanish Franciscan fathers who founded a series of missions from San Diego in the south to Sonoma in the north. They planted an unidentified European grape around the missions, and made both wine and brandy.

By mid-19th century, brandy distilling in California had become an adjunct of the state's developing wine industry. Some California growers, enthralled by cognac's eminence, imported Folle Blanche and Colombard vines from the Charente and tried to duplicate the noble spirit. Although the brandy they made was popular in the old West—perhaps even more so than whiskey—Americans generally did not respond to it. In any case, the brandy industry came to a dead stop with Prohibition.

California brandy production got off to a creaking start after Repeal, with initial efforts again aimed at imitating cognac. Some producers even called their product by that esteemed name; French government protests ended the practice almost immediately. Before long, however, California brandy producers realized that their product should be uniquely American rather than an ersatz cognac. With help from the brandy sages at the University of California Department of Viticulture and Oenology, they committed themselves to making a brandy true to its origins.

HOW CALIFORNIA BRANDY IS MADE

The principal grape varieties used in California brandy include the Thompson seedless, Tokay, and Emperor, plus small amounts of five or six other grapes. Most grow in the lush San Joaquin valley, down through the center of the state.

The brandy is distilled from specially made young wines. Most of it goes through continuous stills, although a small amount of pot still brandy is made, mainly for blending purposes. The continuous still brandy runs off at close to 170°, a fairly light, clean distillate. After reduction to 135°, the brandy goes into American oak barrels for a minimum of 2 years, but in most cases 4. Since producers desire lightness, they age in previously used or charred new barrels, employing large cooperage to avoid excessive woodiness.

Most brandies are rectified with a bit of caramel for color and a trace of sweetening or fruit extract for smoothness. A small category, called "straight," is totally free of any rectifying material except caramel for color. Most California brandies are 80°.

Excellent mixed with juices or soda, and sipped on-the-rocks, but this light, clean brandy is not really meant for the snifter.

INSIDER'S GUIDE TO
CALIFORNIA BRANDY

California brandy is often touted for its mixability because it is low-key and unassertive. Generally speaking, California brandy can be described as clean, light, and smooth, with an appealing flowery-fruity bouquet and occasionally a perception of sweetness. Most examples are not notably distinctive. The straights are dryer and tend to a slightly fuller, more austere style. The miniscule number of California brandies that are substantially or entirely pot still display greater depth, roundness, and complexity.

California brandy labels are relatively free of stars, letters, and purple prose—none of which offers clues to age or style anyway. Small differences in price among brands are not significant of quality, but any that are noticeably more expensive can be expected to have more age, often a proportion of pot still brandy, and greater individuality.

Standard California Brandies

BRANDS ▶

Christian Brothers: The best-selling label and a typical California brandy; clean, fruity, and light-bodied with a hint of sweetness in the aftertaste.

Coronet: A bit dryer than Christian Brothers.

Korbel and **Paul Masson:** A touch fuller than Christian Brothers.

Other reliable examples of standard California brandies include **Almaden, Aristocrat, Lejon,** and **Old Mr. Boston.**

Straight California Brandies

BRANDS ▶

Ceremony: Dry, full-bodied; a bit oaky.

Conti-Royale: 10 years old; similar in style to Ceremony.

E & J (Gallo): Clean, balanced, well-made; second only to Christian Brothers in popularity.

Setrakian: Fruity and medium-bodied.

Premium California Brandies

BRANDS ▶

Christian Brothers XO: Aged premium brandy; about 50% pot still; fragrant, full-bodied, and complex, with definite oak character.

Woodbury: Recently launched; 100% pot still; along with fruit, it shows vanilla from the oak in both bouquet and taste, but is slightly gruff.

R & S Vineyards California Alambic Brandy: Not yet on the market; the product of a joint venture by Schramsberg Vineyards of the Napa Valley and Rémy-Martin of Cognac. The new company will distill Napa-grown grapes in pot stills imported from France, and will age the brandy in Limousin oak barrels.

Application: California brandy bills itself as "the one bottle bar," suggesting that the product can be used for virtually any mixed drink. That, of course, is a matter of taste, but it is certainly fine for such classic brandy cocktails as the Stinger and the Sidecar. It also substitutes nicely in standard whiskey drinks, mates well with fruit juices, and is appealing in coffee drinks. The more distinguished, aged examples are rewarding taken neat or over ice.

Brandies of Spain

Although a substantial percentage of Spanish brandy is *finished* in the sherry-growing region around Jerez, in southwestern Spain, it is, in fact, made from wines of other regions. Sherry itself is too costly to be diverted to spirits. The wines destined to be brandy are first distilled in continuous stills and then shipped to Jerez for aging in old sherry barrels.

Spanish brandy shippers follow the sherry-making practice of maturing in *solera,* an ongoing system of blending older and younger brandies: barrels of brandy are stacked 3 or 4 high, according to age, with the youngest examples at the top and the oldest at the bottom. Brandy for bottling is drawn from the casks in the lowest tier, but they are never completely emptied. The vacated space is immediately filled with brandies from the barrels in the tier above, and these in turn are topped up from the tier above them. The system makes for uniformity within a given style or quality of brandy. Sherry-region brandies tend to be a touch sweet, somewhat woody, fragrant, and full-bodied. Major sherry houses—**Duff-Gordon, Gonzalez-Byass, Pedro Domecq, Sandeman,** and **Terry**—also market a range of brandies.

Torres, a winery in the Penedes region of northeastern Spain near Barcelona, makes a somewhat different style of brandy. Torres uses pot stills, and while the brandies are aged in a *solera,* the barrels are Limousin oak. Their brandies are dry and balanced, lighter than those from Jerez.

Among themselves, Spaniards often refer to brandy as either *coñac* or *aguardiente.* While it is obvious that the first of these unofficial designations is inaccurate, the second is no more correct. *Aguardiente,* actually a name for pomace brandy (page 68), is used loosely for almost any distilled spirit made in Spain.

Brandies of Italy

Since Italy produces a veritable river of wine, it is perfectly logical that brandy is made there as well. The Italian brandy that is exported is on the light side and not totally dry. Made from sound wines, it is distilled in continuous stills and aged in oak containers—all under government supervision.

Vecchia Romagna VSOP, Carpene Malvolti and **Stock:** are among the leading export brands. Distillerie Stock maintains extensive brandy distilling operations outside of Italy and claims that when total international production is included, Stock is the largest-selling brandy in the world.

Brandies of Other Countries

Brandy is exported in varying quantities from a number of other wine-producing countries. With few exceptions, they are column still brandies, perfectly palatable but of no particular distinction.

Portugal

Both table wine and port producers make brandy, known as *aguardente,* which is similar to Spanish but a bit dryer. During World War II, when French brandies were not available, Portuguese brandies were sold to the U.K. and the U.S. in sizeable quantities, but their export has since diminished. **Macieira** is one of the few brands currently in the export market.

Greece

Greek brandies are generally made in pot stills and aged in oak casks. They are quite full, with an ameliorating touch of sweetness. **Metaxa:** The most famous Greek spirit; often regarded as a brandy, but technically a liqueur since it is both flavored and sweetened, albeit lightly; made from a base of pot still brandy; well-aged.

Israel
Carmel, the main export brand, is a fruity, fairly light, (and kosher) column still brandy, made by the largest wine cooperative in Israel.

Germany
German grapes are too expensive to distill, so the majority of German *weinbrands* are made of wines imported from Mediterranean countries. Most are distilled in column stills. **Asbach-Uralt:** Possibly Germany's finest brandy; double distilled in large pot stills; smooth, balanced, and somewhat lighter than cognac.

Mexico
Mexican brandy has become very popular in the home market in recent years, where it now outsells tequila. Distilled in column stills and aged by the *solera* method, it is flavorful and slightly sweet—heavier than California brandy. **Presidente Brandy:** Typical of Mexican brandy, and the leading brand.

South America
Such brandy as is made in South American wine-producing countries is, for the most part, consumed locally. *Pisco* is the best-known type of brandy made in South America. It is generally conceded to have originated in Peru, but is now made in Chile as well. Most pisco is made from muscat grapes and double distilled in pot stills. Aged briefly, it is fragrant, clear, and a bit coarse. Peru exports a brand called **Inca Pisco.** Pisco is taken in drinks such as the Pisco Punch and Pisco Sour, or mixed with fruit juices.

Pomace Brandies
Brandy made from the pomace remaining after grapes have been pressed for wine is found in many countries under a variety of names. The mash (or mess) of grape skins, seeds, and, sometimes, stems is fermented and distilled, producing a tingly, leathery, often rough spirit with its own singular appeal. When it comes to pomace brandies, there is no in-between; people either love or hate them.

Marc, from France, is made all over the country, but in rather small quantities, and the bulk of it is consumed locally, without aging—true firewater! However, there are a few marcs that have enough potential to warrant aging and bottling. Most of these are made from pomace that is *égrappé*—free of the stems that add the harshest flavor notes. Some of the finer **marcs de Bourgogne** (Burgundy), for instance, are the product of such famous Burgundy vineyards as Clos de Tart and the Domaine de la Romanée-Conti. They are distilled in pot stills and aged in small oak casks for several years. These marcs develop roundness and complexity, although they never totally lose the characteristic woodsy-straw taste. **Marc de Champagne,** from the sparkling wine region, is made in a special type of pot still and aged in wood. It is somewhat lighter and more aromatic than marc from Burgundy, but shows some rankness.

Possibly the most distinctive marc comes from Alsace, made from the pomace of the spicy gewürztraminer grape. **Marc de gewürztraminer** is distilled twice in pot stills and aged in ceramic or glass rather than wood containers so that it remains colorless. It is more distinctive than other marcs, retaining some of the spicy-perfumey character of the gewürztraminer grape.

Marcs are only randomly exported, and the brands may vary; but any that turn up from the wine regions previously merit investigation by brandy aficionados.

Grappa, from Italy, is produced and drunk throughout the country. A lot of it—distilled purely for local consumption—is colorless, raw, and harsh. The better examples, distilled from cleaner pomace and given some age, have a grain-like aroma and taste. Flavored grappas and grappa specialties abound in Italy but are seldom exported. While some grappas are aged in steel tanks and remain colorless, those that are wood-aged acquire a bit of color and are softer and rounder. Grappas with extra age are labelled *stravecchio.* Not a great deal of grappa is exported, but occasional bottles of **Stock Grappa** and **Carpene Malvolti Grappa Classico** do turn up. Grappa fanciers enjoy it with coffee, in coffee, or from a just-emptied, warm coffee cup.

Aguardiente from Spain and *bagaceira* from Portugal are other examples of pomace brandies. They are seldom seen outside their native lands.

Fruit Brandies

Perhaps the most ingratiating of all brandies are those made from fruit other than grapes. In effect, they concentrate and store the heady flavors and bouquets of the fruits from which they are distilled. These dry, austere, intensely fragrant *eaux de vie* are colorless; in fact, they are often referred to as *alcools blanc*—white alcohols. (Apple brandies are the only major exception; they are described on page 73.) Fruit brandies run between 80° and 90°—and at one time tended to 100°—in contrast to "fruit-flavored" brandies, which are 70°.

The abundance of fruit that grows around the upper reaches of the Rhine river—including Alsace in northeastern France, Germany's Black Forest, and northern Switzerland—has made this a prime area for the production of *eaux de vie.* There are also a few examples from middle European countries.

HOW FRUIT BRANDIES ARE MADE

There is no single method for making fruit brandies, but there are certain common threads. Fruit brandies require substantial amounts of fresh fruit in relation to the quantity of spirits they yield. Different producers give varying estimates as to the amount of fruit needed for a given brandy, but it is safe to say that it can take 25 pounds of fruit, or more, to make a bottle of *eau de vie.*

Each step in the production of a fruit brandy is designed to heighten the bouquet. Only the ripest fruit is used, for maximum fragrance and flavor. For "stone" fruits—those with large pits, such as plums or cherries—the pits are included in the mash. However, care is taken not to crush them—at least for the finer brandies—since that would release undesired bitter-almond flavors. In fact, a definite perception of almond is a characteristic of less carefully made *eau de vie.*

Except in the case of berries, the mash of fruit is fermented into a kind of wine, which is then distilled. A double distillation takes place when pot stills are used, a single distillation for continuous stills. Berries, which lack sufficient sugar for proper fermentation, are steeped in high-proof spirits until all their exquisite taste and scent have been extracted. The infusion is then distilled once, even when a pot still is used. Regardless of the method of distillation, most fruit brandies run off the still at fairly low proofs.

Unlike other brandies, the *alcools blanc* are not aged in wood—wood would impart color, and introduce a distracting taste. Glass or glass-lined containers have traditionally been used for aging, but stainless steel tanks are now increasingly employed. In any case, fruit brandies are not usually aged for very long before bottling. The idea is to smooth out some of the rough edges without sacrificing the freshness of the fruit fragrance.

INSIDER'S GUIDE TO FRUIT BRANDIES

While dozens of fruits are made into brandy, some are produced in such small quantities that they are never seen outside their own locale. One such is **houx,** made in Alsace from holly berries. **Houx** has a rather vegetal aroma and taste and is interesting mainly as a curiosity. The following fruit brandies are more available.

Kirsch, made from wild cherries, is the most familiar of the fruit *eaux de vie.* Its bouquet and flavor reflect the fruit, and often a faint almond undertone imparted by the pits. French kirsch is generally lighter than the German and Swiss examples, which are called **Kirschwasser.**

Poire, made from the William pear, similar to the Bartlett has a full, intense ripe pear bouquet, although the taste is not quite as fruity as the aroma. Occasionally one sees a bottle of *poire* that contains a whole pear. Originally, this was accomplished by slipping the empty bottle over a blossom or tiny immature fruit on a pear tree branch. With luck, the pear would develop to full size within the bottle, which would then be filled with pear brandy. These days, it is likely to be done an easier way: the pear is inserted into a bottle that has no bottom; the bottom is then fused on and the brandy poured in. It is questionable how much flavor the pear in the bottle adds, but it's certainly a conversation piece.

Framboise (called **Himbeergeist** in Germany and parts of Switzerland), made from raspberries, is extremely fragrant, with the appealing perfume of lushly ripe fruit. The taste is dry and hints delicately of the berry.

Mirabelle, made from a small yellow plum, is produced mostly in France. Its fragrance and taste are pleasingly fruity, though not as distinctive as **framboise** or **poire.** There are two other plum brandies worth mentioning: **Quetsch,** made from blue plums in France, Germany and Switzerland, is similar to **mirabelle,** but possibly a little fuller; **slivovitz,** made from the blue sljiva plum in Yugoslavia and other eastern European countries, is aged in wood, which imparts a straw or pale gold color. Because of the wood aging, it is less fruity and more brandy-like than other plum *eaux de vie.*

Barack Palinka, made from apricots in Austria and Hungary, has the scent of apricots with some almond fragrance. The apricot is experienced as much in the finish, or after-taste, as in the taste itself.

   FRUIT BRANDY
BUYING GUIDE

BRANDS ▶
The houses of **Trimbach, Jean Danflou** (France), **Schladerer** (Germany), and **Dettling** (Switzerland) each offer a comprehensive selection of fruit brandies.
Brana (France) makes an appealing *eau de vie de poire.*
Baron de Braux (France) produces *Mirabelle de Lorraine* in small quantities; it has a lovely fragrance.
Zwack (Austria) is noted for its *Barack Palinka.*

Application: Unlike other brandies, fruit brandies are most pleasing served lightly chilled. Their pronounced fragrance is minimally affected by cold, while the rather dry, somewhat alcoholic taste is smoothed and softened by chilling. For some, chilling the glasses only—not the bottle— is sufficient. Ice *in* the glass is a matter of taste, although frowned on by aficionados.

Tulip-shaped glasses are preferred, and not the smallest size. They should be large enough to allow the bouquet to develop, and stemmed so that the hand is not in contact with the bowl of the glass. The best way to enjoy the fragrance is to put the nose in the top of the glass and sniff briefly. Too deep a breath might be overpowering. *Eaux de vie* are pleasing after-dinner *digestifs,* and they can be taken as aperitifs as well. They are delightful, too, poured over lightly sweetened fresh fruit. A German saying covers it all: "You should drink *eau de vie* when you're not feeling so well, and also—when you're feeling well."

LE TROU NORMAND

The food of Normandy is traditionally rich, hearty, and copious—based on the local thick cream, butter, cheeses, seafood, flavorful *pré-salé* lamb, fine poultry, and fruit. The canny Normans have, however, developed their own way of dealing with this abundance—*le trou Normand,* or Norman hole. This is a shot of young Calvados, ceremonially downed midpoint in the meal, which purportedly creates room for the courses to follow. It may not be scientific, but the Normans swear by it.

Apple Brandies

There are two major types of apple brandy—**calvados** from France and **applejack** from the U.S.—that are made differently from other fruit *eaux de vie.*

INSIDER'S GUIDE TO APPLE BRANDIES

Calvados comes from Normandy in northwestern France and, as with cognac and armagnac, the geographical limits and details of production are regulated by French law. The finest calvados bears the *appellation contrôlée* Pays d'Auge and is produced in a small area around the seaside resort of Deauville. The apples that grow there are not much to look at nor to taste, yet they make the best brandy. The apples are crushed and fermented into cider, which is then double-distilled in pot stills. Most calvados, however, bears a lesser classification—*appellation réglementée.* This is made in 10 designated areas that form a rough semicircle around the Pays d-Auge. Some *réglementée* is made in pot stills, but most goes through a single distillation in a continuous still.

All calvados is aged in oak casks, acquiring color, subtlety, and mellowness. While it begins to display finesse after 4 or 5 years in wood, some calvados is aged for decades. Calvados matures more slowly than other brandies, since the proof is not reduced prior to

CALVADOS REGION

Calvados, situated in the ancient province of Normandy, is famed for its superior apple brandy to which it gives its name.

barreling. Almost all calvados is a blend of several years and is bottled at between 80° and 86°.

Calvados evokes the fragrance and flavor of apples, particularly marked in younger brandies. In addition to the forthright fresh apple taste and aroma, young calvados is raw and hot. Older calvados still hints of apple, but wood and time refine the bouquet and taste, making it more complex and mellow—closer to mature brandies made from grapes.

Connoisseurs are partial to *appellation côntrolée* Pays d'Auge. But it must be said that some *appellation réglementée* compares favorably to the Pays d'Auge. *Réglementée* tends to be lighter, cleaner, and less intense than Pays d'Auge, especially when young.

Calvados labels bear stars, letters, and names that are reminiscent of cognac and armagnac, with the following age minimums for the youngest brandy in the blend: three stars or apples—two years old; Réserve or Vieux—3 years old; VO or Vieille Réserve—4 years old; VSOP or Grand Réserve—5 years old; Extra Napoleon, Hors d'Age, or Age Inconnu—more than 5 years. But such a variety of names is used on calvados labels that they are not always a clear guide to age level. The label *will* indicate if the calvados is *appellation contrôlée* Pays d'Auge or *appellation réglementée*. Consumers should be aware that some brands offer both styles. In any case, price is a clue. Exported calvados is usually Réserve level or higher, and there is a price jump of about 50% from level to level.

CALVADOS
BUYING GUIDE

BRANDS ▶
All are 80° unless otherwise noted.
Appellation contrôlée **Pays d'Auge**
Boulard Fine, Ducs de Normandie Vieux, and **Ecusson Carte d'Or Vieux** (84°): Younger calvados, with fresh apple aroma and taste; still rough, with a perception of alcohol in the finish.
Boulard Grande Fine, Ducs de Normandie Vieille Réserve, and **Père Magloire Grande Fine VSOP:** Older, have nuances of oak along with a more complex apple fragrance and flavor; smooth, although the **Ducs de Normandie** has not lost all of its bite.
Bizouard and **Busnel Hors d'Age** (86°): Well-aged, showing rich apple-oak bouquet and taste; complex, smooth, and dry, with a long finish.
Appellation réglementée **calvados**
Calvados Montgommery: Modest apple taste, somewhat masked by medicinal woody notes and a noticeably sweet finish.
La Pommeraie and **Père Magloire:** Fresh apple aroma and taste; clean and fairly smooth.

Application: Young calvados may be used in mixed drinks, much like California brandy. Older calvados is best taken neat, the way one would enjoy the more distinguished brandies.

COLONIAL APPLEJACK
Despite applejack's New Jersey associations, there is one piece of applejack lore that has a New England origin. It is said that the first applejack made there was not distilled at all. Instead, a cask of fermented or "hard" cider would be buried in a snowbank during the winter. The water fraction of the cider would freeze, while the alcohol would remain liquid—a reverse of the distillation principle. A hot poker pushed through the bung hole of the cask would clear an opening, releasing the spiritous "jack."

Applejack, according to a unanimous resolution passed by the New Jersey Senate in 1964, is "the oldest native distilled spirit beverage in the United States." Although applejack may be made anywhere in the United States, much of its early history is New Jersey–connected. And Laird's—for all practical purposes, the only applejack distillery now in operation—is located in that state.

Most applejack on the market today is a blend of no less than 20% apple brandy; the rest is neutral spirits. The apple brandy portion is distilled from hard cider and must be aged in oak containers at least 2 years. Such a blend is not redolent of apple flavor; it is a light, fairly bland spirit with a modicum of apple fruitiness. Laird's makes a small amount of *straight* applejack—unblended and 100°—and that has definite apple flavor and fragrance.

Application: Same as for calvados.

Medaillon is Martell's proprietary name for its VSOP Cognac. There are a number of other fine VSOP Cognacs, but only one Medaillon.

GLOSSARY

ALCOOLS BLANC: "White alcohols"—a French term for fruit brandies that retain their clear color because they are not aged in wood.

ALEMBIC or **ALAMBIC:** The name given to pot stills in France and other European countries.

APPELLATION CONTRÔLÉE: "Controlled designation." When these words appear on the label of a French spirit (or wine), it is a legal guarantee that the item was produced in a specified manner and in a particular geographical area. It is *not* a guarantee of quality.

AQUA VITAE: "Water of life," an early name given to spirits.

EAU DE VIE: Originally the same as *aqua vitae* (see above). Now used as a generic term for colorless fruit brandy.

FINE: (pronounced *feen*). A generic term for brandy in France.

GRAPPA: Italian name for brandy distilled from *pomace* (see below).

MARC: French name for brandy distilled from *pomace* (see below).

POMACE: Crushed skins, seeds, and stems left after grapes have been pressed for wine.

VIGNERON: French name for wine-grower.

WEINBRAND: German name for brandy; literally, "burnt wine."

Clear Spirits

ALL SPIRITS are clear when they run off the still. Color comes later, by extraction from the cask during aging, by the addition of caramel, or—in the case of liqueurs—by the use of food dyes. However, for the clear spirits, aging or the cosmetic application of color is not required for palatability.

A number of spirits are bottled colorless and unaged. Fruit brandies, previously described on pages 70–76, are one example. But the major categories of clear spirits—gin, aquavit, and, most prevalent, vodka—are usually distilled primarily from grain.

Vodka and aquavit are primarily associated with northern Europe. In their beginnings, when they were distilled in primitive alembics from any available carbohydrates, they could not have been very appealing. So it may legitimately be asked why the practice of aging, used in other places, was not employed. The rigorous climate of northeastern Europe and Scandinavia may have been a factor; perhaps it was just too cold to wait around for the spirits to mellow in wooden barrels. As for gin, which came into the picture somewhat later, it was mainly a drink for the poor, who could not afford the luxury of aged spirits. Eventually, of course, improved production methods and quality controls for all the clear spirits allowed them to develop the singular character for which each is appreciated today.

Vodka

Vodka is essentially neutral spirits and, considering how simple it is, a surprising number of myths surround it. Possibly the most persistent is that it is made from potatoes. Although it can be distilled from just about anything fermentable, most vodkas are made from grain.

Not more than thirty years ago, vodka was an obscure spirit everywhere except in its native habitat, eastern Europe. So its recent rise to world popularity and best-selling spirit status in the U.S. is one of the legends of the liquor industry. The story began in the 1930s when the Heublein Company acquired the U.S. rights to the Smirnoff brand. At the time, Americans perceived vodka as a vaguely sinister spirit. What knowledge they had of it came mainly from movies about old Russia, in which vodka drinkers invariably ended up under the table. The earliest inkling of vodka's future came in 1939 when a South Carolina distributor hesitantly bought 25 cases of Smirnoff, reserving the right to return them if they did not sell. Instead, there was a second order for 50 cases, soon followed by another for 100 more.

It turned out that an enterprising salesman in the territory had sampled the strange new product and, finding it colorless and relatively free of flavor and aroma, made up advertising streamers that read, "Smirnoff White Whiskey. No taste. No smell." He hung them in stores and almost immediately, curious customers began buying the stuff. Investigation revealed that they were mixing it with cola, milk, whatever they liked to drink, since vodka takes on the flavor of the mixer. But before Smirnoff could exploit this stunning insight, World War II effectively shut down vodka production for several years. It was not until the early 1950s that Smirnoff launched its highly successful advertising campaign on vodka's versatility. It was a classic example of the right product at the right time and place. Vodka lent itself to easy, moderate, pleasant drinking—at the moment when a post-Depression, postwar U.S. was starting to learn about the good life.

Obviously, the vodka bonanza could not remain the property of a single company for very long, and the shelves of American liquor stores were quickly crowded with dozens of new domestic brands—followed by the importation of "authentic" vodkas from Russia and Poland. Vodka's acceptance became international, and because it is simple to formulate, vodka is now produced globally.

WHO INVENTED VODKA

The question of where vodka was first made has produced a monumental public relations battle between the Soviet Union and Poland, with strong and definite assertions by each side.

A Soviet source thunders "Russia is the true native land of vodka. The word vodka also appears to be purely Russian. In the opinions of not only Soviet scientists and linguists but also Polish and German philologists, 'vodka' appears to be a derivative of the Russian word 'voda' (water), to which the diminutive 'k' has been added."

A Polish spokesperson, on the other hand, contends, "As a matter of historical fact, vodka originated in Poland! The diminutive word 'wodka' (from the Polish word for water: 'woda') passed from the Polish into the Russian language as late as the 19th century. This was stated, among others, by the famous philologist, Professor Alexander Bruckner, from the Berlin University, in his 'Etymological Dictionary of the Polish language.' Before that, the Russian language, properly speaking, had no 'wodka' word!"

There have also been mutterings on vodka's beginnings from the Irish, Arabs, and, recently, the Chinese. But vodka is, after all, a basic distillate and probably "original" to a number of geographic areas: a phenomenon known among anthropologists as cultural parallelism.

HOW VODKA IS MADE

There are differences from country to country and from producer to producer, in the variety of grain (or, rarely, other material) used to make vodka, but it is always the most available and economical. As with whiskey, the grain is made into a mash, fermented, and then put through a continuous still—the universal method for vodka. The distillate comes off somewhere around 190°, almost entirely free of the congeners that contribute distinctive flavor elements to whiskeys.

The new spirit may then be run through a filtering substance, such as charcoal, or be minimally rectified. After being reduced with water, usually to 80° or 100°, it is bottled without aging.

THE ICE JACKET

For important occasions, a vodka or aquavit bottle may be encased in an ice jacket—which makes a dramatic presentation and keeps the contents frigid. Here's how to do it: Pour about half an inch of water into an empty half-gallon milk container or 46-ounce juice can; freeze. Center the bottle on the frozen base and add water to just below the shoulder of the bottle; freeze. To release the jacket, dip the container quickly in hot water and slide it off. Place the bottle on a tray to catch the drippings. When pouring, wrap the bottle in a napkin to keep your fingers from freezing.

INSIDER'S GUIDE TO VODKA

Vodka certainly does not have bold flavor, but neither is it as totally tasteless as producers would like us to believe. All vodkas have the aroma and taste of ethanol (alcohol). Nor is it true that vodka "leaves you breathless." The scent of alcohol does linger on the breath—albeit lightly—after vodka has been imbibed.

European vodkas in general are not as cleanly made as the U.S. versions. The European vodkas come off the still at slightly lower proofs and are rectified more often than not—sometimes with a little glycerin for smoothness, or with a trace of sugar or other flavor enhancer. Because of this, they tend to show subtle taste differences among themselves. U.S.-made vodkas are more uniform in character.

United States Vodka

In the keen competition among vodka brands on the market, advertising claims of outstanding dryness, clarity, and refinement are routine. However, laboratory analysis reveals only minimal differences among U.S. vodkas, since all must conform to federal requirements that they be "neutral spirits so distilled, or so treated after distillation with charcoal or other materials, as to be without distinctive character, aroma, taste, or color." *Distinctive* is the operative word here. Charcoal, incidentally, is not used much these days. Modern distilling equipment and techniques are so precise that the desired neutrality is obtainable without filtering.

When a number of U.S. vodka brands are sampled head to head, tasters may observe differences among them, but in practical terms, the variations are not significant. Since U.S. vodkas are used primarily in mixed drinks, whatever individuality they might have is obliterated by the flavor of other ingredients. So it makes sense to buy by price rather than by brand image. U.S. vodkas are generally offered in 80° and 100°.

★   **U.S. VODKA**   ★
BUYING GUIDE

BRANDS ▶
Smirnoff: By far the leading brand in the U.S.; comes in a range of proofs. The line also includes the atypical **Smirnoff de Czar** (82.6°)—formulated in the style of European vodkas that are drunk cold and neat; made to have a hint of flavor and leave a somewhat oilier, smoother tactile impact than standard U.S. vodkas; although it would seem that it departs from the standards of identity for vodka (mentioned above), the rules are apparently flexible enough to allow for the addition of minimal flavor substances.
The Heublein Company, which makes Smirnoff, also makes **Popov** and **Relska.**
   Gilbey's, Gordon's, Kamchatka, and **Wolfschmidt** are other leading vodka brands.
   Local brands and private labels too numerous to mention here—are also widely available and attractively priced.
    Everclear (190°): A grain alcohol that advertises itself as "twice the spirit of vodka," with the suggestion that half the amount be used in vodka-type drinks. While one's appreciation of the product is a matter of taste, it does have more bite than 80° to 100° vodkas, even when half as much is used.
    Tvarski Double Vodka (160°): Somewhat similar to Everclear.

Application: U.S. vodkas shine in such drinks as the Bloody Mary, Screwdriver, Bullshot, Gimlet, Martini, and Black Russian, or with juices, tonic, and other carbonated mixers—in fact, with almost anything. They can also be poured over rocks, with a twist. The extra-high proofs mentioned above are useful in punches and homemade cordials and when steeped with fruit.

Russian and Polish Vodkas

The Warsaw Pact notwithstanding, Russia and Poland each unequivocally claims the invention of vodka some 600 to 1000 years ago, and it is an argument as murky as whether *uisquebaugh* originated in Scotland or Ireland. Whatever the case, vodka is the national drink of both countries, and despite the proliferation of U.S. examples, Russia and Poland set the standard for vodka in the world. Russian vodka's eminence, in particular, is implicitly acknowledged by the prevalence of the Russian-sounding names given to vodkas made elsewhere.

Vodkas of varying qualities and styles are distilled in both countries for the domestic market, but for the most part, each exports only one or two major brands.

Russia is synonymous with vodka, and Stolichnaya is synonymous with Russian vodka. An excellent choice for drinking neat; less expensive vodkas make more sense for mixing in cocktails and tall drinks.

Soviet Union

Stolichnaya and **Moskovaya** are the main exported brands. The former is available in the U.S., the latter in Canada, while both can be found in the U.K. These vodkas have smooth, almost silky body and a faint sweetness. **Stoli** is a bit cleaner than **Moskovaya;** its bottlings for the U.S. are at both 80° and 100°.

Poland

Wyborowa Wodka (the *w* is pronounced *v*) is distilled from rye grain and bottled at both 80° and 100°. It is firm-bodied and crisply dry, with a barely perceptible tang.

Application: The subtle flavors offered by Russian and Polish vodkas can only be appreciated if they are taken straight or on the rocks—and preferably the former. Once combined with orange juice, tomato juice, or other popular vodka mixers, their unique quality is buried. If your drink is a Bloody Mary, it is a waste to use Stoli or Wyborowa. The only possible exception might be in a *very* dry Martini (say 11 to 0).

The traditional way to drink Russian and Polish vodkas is to down them neat and frigid. Bottles are routinely stored in the refrigerator and frequently in the freezer. In the latter case, the vodka attains a syrupy consistency. The icy vodka is usually served in thin liqueur glasses; occasionally, a grind of black pepper is added. The pepper particles slowly float down, adding visual interest as well as taste.

Flavored Vodkas

These are popular in the Soviet Union, where literally dozens are available. Those listed below are exported, albeit in limited quantities.

BRANDS ▶

Limonnaya (70°): Lemon-flavored and slightly sweetened; more lemon scent than taste.

Okhotnichya (90°): "Hunter's vodka"; seasoned with meadow grasses and heather honey; aromatic and spicy.

Pertsovka (70°): Flavored with pepper; hot and snappy, it makes a Bloody Mary that requires no further seasoning.

Starka (86°): Flavored with fruit leaves, brandy, and port wine; vaguely brandy-like.

Zubrovka (U.S.S.R.) and **Zubrowka** (Poland) are enchanting flavored vodkas. They are steeped with buffalo grass, and each bottle contains a blade of the fragrant green. They offer the evocative scent of new-mown hay, and in the case of Poland's **Polmos Zubrowka,** a hint of almonds in the aftertaste. Regrettably, neither may be imported into the U.S. at present, because some of the flavoring ingredients are in technical violation of government regulations. It is possible that the rather esoteric requirements may be accommodated in the future so that these delightful items will once again be available in the States.

Vodkas of Other Countries

Except where noted, the vodkas listed below are produced from grain and bottled at 80°. A number are also available at higher proofs: Check labels. Several are handsomely packaged, heightening their cachet as "imports." While these vodkas can be used in mixed drinks, they are also enjoyable chilled and neat, or on the rocks.

Canada

Clean, dry **Silhouette** is closer to U.S. vodkas than those from other parts of the world.

China

Great Wall and **Tsing Tao** have a slightly perfumey fragrance and taste.

England

Burrough's English Vodka (91.5°) has smooth body, good mouth feel, and touches of both salt and sweetness in the finish. The same basic vodka is offered under the **Borzoi** label in England, at 80° and 100°.

Israel

Anatevka and **Carmel** are derived from grapes, not grain. They have a slight bite and are not totally dry. Both are kosher.

Japan

Suntory Vodka has a style that is midway between the more flavorful eastern European vodkas and the almost tasteless American. It comes in a lovely, square, stylized bottle.

Scandinavia

Absolut from Sweden and **Finlandia** from Finland have a touch more body and flavor than American vodkas. They are clean, dry, and pleasing, but with no special taste distinction. Both come in attractive bottles.

Sermeq from Denmark takes its name from the Eskimo word for glacier, to emphasize the fact that its water content comes from the Greenland ice cap. Infusions of arctic plants are alleged to give it special character; we noted a hint of citrus—but nothing more.

Gin

The name "gin" comes from *genièvre,* French for "juniper," and the one characteristic all gins share is the presence of the juniper berry as a major flavoring ingredient.

Franciscus de la Boe, a professor of medicine at the University of Leyden in Holland, is credited with formulating the first gin about 300 years ago. His orientation was medicinal, since juniper berries were valued for their therapeutic properties, as were the distilled spirits in which they were infused. But whatever appeal *genever*—the Dutch name—had as a nostrum was soon overshadowed by its popularity as a beverage.

British troops fighting in the Low Countries discovered that a tot of this aromatic potion before the fracas miraculously transformed them into 17th-century John Waynes. They happily took the "Dutch Courage" back to England, anglicizing the name "gin" en route. Gin was cheap and easy to make, and consumption grew enormously in England during the 18th and 19th centuries, particularly among the urban poor. Hogarth's famous depiction of the squalor and degradation of "Gin Lane" shows this sign over the doorway of a gin shop: "Drunk for a penny/ Dead drunk for twopence/ Clean straw for Nothing"—which neatly sums up the nature of many gins of the period.

Periodic attempts by the British government to curtail or ban the production and sale of gin—as in the Gin Act of 1736—simply spurred the production of illicit gin, marketed under such fanciful names as Cuckold's Comfort, Last Shift, Royal Poverty, and My Lady's Eye Water. Almost two centuries later, Prohibition in the U.S. had a similar effect—the appearance of a bootleg spirit known as "bathtub gin." It was made by mixing raw alcohol, oil of juniper, assorted aromatics, and distilled water in a large container—sometimes in a bathtub, hence the name. Not only were these illegal gins of dubious quality, but they were often dangerous, and the desire to remove them from circulation was one of the factors leading to the repeal of *both* the Gin Act and Prohibition.

Modern gin was introduced in the latter half of the 19th century when several London distillers began to make a refined, nonsweet gin quite unlike either the heavy-bodied Holland *genevers* or the "Gin Lane" types, which were heavily flavored and sweetened to mask their obvious flaws. The new style became known as "London Dry" (or simply "Dry"), the prototype of gins now produced in the

U.K. and the U.S. and by far the leading type in the world. Gin's popularity was enhanced by its mixable quality: It quickly became an ingredient in many of the new cocktails that came into fashion at the turn of the century, and reached new heights during the Prohibition era.

HOW GIN IS MADE

Today's gin starts off with high proof spirits, usually distilled from grain. They are then redistilled with or over juniper berries, citrus peels, cassia bark, angelica root, anise, coriander seeds, and other botanicals. Compound gin, a simple mixture of distilled spirits and botanical extracts, is the least costly to make. But the method is also the least satisfactory, and compounds are no longer much of a factor in the gin market. Like vodka, gin needs no aging, nor does it usually receive any. Once the gin has been reduced to bottling proof, it is ready to be sold.

The base spirits used in England are of slightly lower proof than are those used in the U.S., and not quite as clean. U.K. distillers prefer to "leave something in the spirit to hang the botanicals on."

OLD TOM GIN

Old Tom, a lightly sweetened gin popular in 18th-century England, has earned a niche in merchandising history as the first vending machine spirit. An ingenious device consisting of a wooden sign in the form of a black cat was nailed below the window of a tavern. The customer deposited one or two pence in the cat's mouth and put his lips to a pipe under the cat's paw. The publican inside then poured a jolt of gin through the pipe and on down the customer's gullet. One need not be a language expert to see the origin of such expressions as "feeding the kitty" and "cat's paw."

Old Tom is the only surviving example of early English gin types. It can occasionally be found in liquor shops that handle esoteric items.

INSIDER'S GUIDE TO GIN

Beyond the basic juniper flavor, gins have an herby-flowery-woodsy taste, reflecting the array of botanicals used. Each distillery has its own closely guarded formula for the types and proportions of flavorings in its gin. Part of gin's attraction is the subtle sensory shading found among the various bottlings. As a rule, British gins are fragrant, intense, and full flavored. U.S. gins are lighter and crisper, with a muted juniper flavor, and more citrus accents. They are also lower in proof; most are 80°, while British gins tend to be over 90°, adding to their assertiveness.

Originally, the term "London Dry" was a geographic appellation—like Cognac for brandy. It referred to the place of origin and a particular style. Today, most gins are made in the London Dry style, regardless of their place of origin.

★   **GIN**   ★
BUYING GUIDE

Britain
BRANDS ▶
Beefeater (94°): Clean, balanced, and smooth; pleasing citrus-juniper flavor; subtle; the top import.
Bombay (86°): More distinct botanical notes; quite dry.
Plymouth (94.4°): Full-bodied and perfumey.
Tanqueray (94.4°): Similar to Beefeater but less subtle; silky body.

United States
All those listed are 80°.
BRANDS ▶
Fleischmann's: Muted and bland.
Gilbey's: Smooth; pleasant juniper flavor.
Gordon's: Similar to Gilbey's, but harsher.
Hiram Walker: Quite muted and bland.
Seagram's Extra Dry. One of the rare aged gins; a pale straw color from several months in wood; smooth, with good juniper flavor.

Germany
Doornkaat (94°) from Frisia and **Jueckemoeller** (80°) from Steinhagen are discreetly flavored, bridging the gap between standard dry gins and vodka.

Application: Gin's major use is still in the Martini, including such variations as the Gibson. Other gin drinks are the Gimlet, Gin and Tonic, Tom Collins, and Rickey. German gins are taken chilled and neat, the way white spirits are ordinarily imbibed in northern Europe. The Frisians still observe their friendly custom of offering guests a welcome drink of chilled Doornkaat in a round-bowled, long-handled pewter spoon. After drinking, one licks the spoon clean so that nothing remains to drip out when the spoon is placed on the table, bowl side down.

Hollands Gin
"Hollands" is the popular name for *genever* (sometimes spelled *jenever*), the gin made in the Netherlands. It is not as full bodied as the early *genevers* but is quite unlike London Dry gin. Hollands is distilled in a pot still from a mash containing a high

proportion of malted barley with other grains—usually rye or corn. It runs off the still at under 110°, thus retaining a good proportion of flavor-giving congeners. Hollands is then redistilled with juniper berries and other botanicals (although fewer than are used for dry gin): the **Bols** brand has a perceptible note of caraway.

The malty, whisky-like notes from the base spirit, added to the juniper flavor, give Hollands a rooty, robust character that would overwhelm the other ingredients if used in cocktails. Instead, Hollands is taken icy cold, neat, in one gulp—often accompanied by the green herring for which Holland is famous.

MARTINI MYTHOLOGY

There is little question that the Martini is the most famous cocktail in the world—the subject of books and innumerable articles. While various theories as to the genesis of the Martini are advanced with utmost certainty, none is absolutely definitive.

John Doxat, in his notable book on the Dry Martini, *Stirred—Not Shaken,* contends that the Martini was invented by Martini di Arma di Taggia, head bartender at the Knickerbocker Hotel in New York City, about 1910. Others assert, just as positively, that the original was the Martinez cocktail, devised in the late 19th century by the legendary American bartender, Professor Jerry Thomas. The Martinez, named for a town in California, was a sweet drink made with Old Tom gin and sweet vermouth—the latter predominating.

In 1949, Bernard DeVoto's article in *Harper's Magazine* proposed a ratio of 3.7 parts gin to 1 part dry vermouth as the precise formula for the perfect Martini. Since then, Martinis have become ever dryer, with proportions that range from 4 to 1 to 30 to 1. Winston Churchill, an authority in these matters, was satisfied with passing the cork from the vermouth bottle over the gin. Martiniphiles concede that such accents as Pernod or Scotch, and such substitutions as vodka for gin or dry sherry for vermouth, may make for pleasing drinks, but they deny that these are true Martinis.

What may be the ultimate Martini comment is made in the story about a backpacker preparing for a foray into high mountain country. He stocked his survival kit with gin, vermouth, and a mixing glass, explaining, "If I'm ever lost, I'll just pour some gin and vermouth into the glass, add a handful of snow, and start stirring. Sure as you're born, someone will show up in two seconds to tell me, 'That's a hell of a way to mix a Martini!' "

Aquavit

Aquavit (also spelled "akvavit" or "akevitt") is Scandinavia's entry in the white spirits derby—and the name is still another word for "water of life." Similar to gin, the prevalent flavor is caraway seed, not juniper.

Like gin, aquavit begins with neutral, high-proof base spirits, with the difference that they may be distilled from potatoes as well as grain. The spirits are then redistilled with flavorings; in addition to the pervasive caraway, other plants such as anise, dill, fennel, and citrus peels are used. With a few exceptions, aquavit is bottled clear and with little or no aging. Aquavits are made in all Scandinavian countries but not many are exported.

"SKOALING"

The classic aquavit toast follows a prescribed ritual. Before downing the spirit, one looks for someone else holding a glass. The first person raises his glass, looks into his partner's eyes, and says "Skoal!" The partner responds in kind. Both drinkers then toss off their aquavits in unison, lower glasses to breast level, and nod to each other. It is considered bad form, however, to "skoal" the hostess; if she had to match drinks with every guest, she might end up as pickled as the herrings in the smorgasbord.

 **AQUAVIT BUYING GUIDE**

Denmark

Aalborg Akvavit (80°): Crisp and smooth; probably the most widely known brand outside Scandinavia. **Aalborg Jubilaeums** (90°): golden, with a definite dill aroma and flavor; exported in limited quantities.

Sweden

Sweden which produces more aquavit than any other Scandinavian country, exports modest amounts of **O.P. Anderson** (80°) which is tinted a pale amber color; dry and fairly full flavored; modest amounts are exported.

Norway

Loiten Akevitt (83°): Untypically aged in oak casks; more full bodied than most.
Linie Akevitt (83°): Fairly dark in color; slightly winey in flavor; its name and character come from being aged in old Madeira casks that cross the equatorial line *(linie)* in the hold of Norwegian ships; not much of it is seen outside of Norway.

Scandinavians prefer their aquavit neat and icy, often followed with a beer chaser.

Germany

Germany, although not a Scandinavian country, does make a notable aquavit. **Bommerlunder Aquavit** (80°): Has a light, mild caraway taste; takes its name from a district in Denmark, a few kilometers from Flensburg, Germany where it is made.

Application: Aquavit is traditionally served very cold; the bottle is often kept in the freezer or encased in an ice jacket. It is taken in small glasses and generally consumed in one gulp, sometimes followed by a beer chaser. On the other hand, Aalborg has been featuring the "Danish Mary"—aquavit mixed with tomato juice—in its advertising. And some bold souls have even suggested that aquavit might be interesting in a Martini! Aquavit is almost always served with food; thus, the following notice, once found in Danish inns: "On these premises aquavit may only be served with rich food. All food is rich—except pancakes. Pancakes may not be served on these premises."

Rum

RUM is a spirit made by fermenting and distilling some form of sugar cane, usually molasses, and is produced in almost every island or area where sugar cane is grown.

Christopher Columbus is most often credited with bringing sugar cane from the Canary Islands to the West Indies on his second voyage to the New World, and it soon became an important crop throughout the Caribbean. Rum was first distilled in that area in the mid-17th century, initially as a way to dispose of excess molasses. The spirit was dispensed to slaves working the cane plantations, to pacify them and relieve their boredom.

Before long, rum won favor with the pirates and privateers who prowled the Caribbean during the 17th century. This gave rise to its wild, yo-ho-ho image, which was later compounded when rum became the official spirit of the British Navy, with a daily ration issued to all hands. As a result, one school holds that the name "rum" came from "rumbullion" or "rumbustion"—old English words meaning rumpus or fracas, presumably the result of over-indulging in the beverage. More sober heads, however, have suggested that the source is the last syllable of the Latin *saccharum*, which means sugar or sweet.

Regardless of its origins, rum developed into a saleable commodity—and an important part of Colonial America's economy as well. Starting in the late 1600s, molasses from the West Indies was shipped to New England, where it was distilled into rum.

Barrels of rum were then shipped from New England to Africa's Gold Coast, where the cargo was bartered for slaves who, in turn, were transported to the West Indies to grow the sugar cane that was made into molasses. This was the infamous triangular trade route, which lasted until slave traffic was finally stopped in the early 19th century. With the elimination of this profitable but shameful arrangement, rum production in the U.S. gradually diminished.

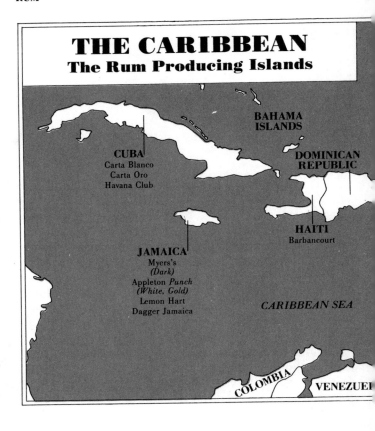

THE CARIBBEAN
The Rum Producing Islands

BAHAMA
ISLANDS

CUBA
Carta Blanco
Carta Oro
Havana Club

DOMINICAN
REPUBLIC

HAITI
Barbancourt

JAMAICA
Myers's
(*Dark*)
Appleton *Punch*
(*White, Gold*)
Lemon Hart
Dagger Jamaica

CARIBBEAN SEA

COLOMBIA

VENEZUE?

Demand declined, too, as whiskey took over as the leading American spirit.

In recent years, however, with the turn to such unassertive potables as vodka, the light-bodied, mixable Puerto Rican rums have taken a leap forward. And now, as the taste pendulum takes its inevitable swing, the more full-bodied rums have started to experience something of a renaissance as well.

INSIDER'S GUIDE TO RUM

Today's rums are classified into two main groups—*light-bodied* and *full-bodied*, each with sub-categories.

Light-bodied rums, made in column stills, tend to be crisp and dry, with subtle flavor and aroma. Most of them have only a hint of molasses character; some rums even approach vodka in neutrality.

Full-bodied rums, made in pot stills, unmistakably proclaim

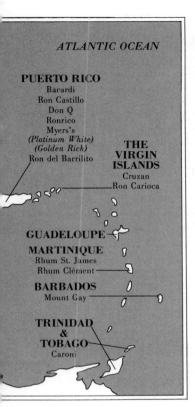

ATLANTIC OCEAN

PUERTO RICO
Bacardi
Ron Castillo
Don Q
Ronrico
Myers's
(Platinum White)
(Golden Rich)
Ron del Barrilito

THE VIRGIN ISLANDS
Cruzan
Ron Carioca

GUADELOUPE

MARTINIQUE
Rhum St. James
Rhum Clément

BARBADOS
Mount Gay

TRINIDAD & TOBAGO
Caroni

Almost every sun-drenched island in the Caribbean produces rum, though not necessarily on a commercial level. The islands and brands listed are most involved in international trade, and therefore most available.

their relationship to sugar cane and molasses. Often perceived as sweet, they are, in fact, not; although they are frankly aromatic, and round and full in the mouth. The "rummy" taste and fragrance associated with such desserts as baba au rhum, Nesselrode pie, and rum-raisin ice cream is characteristic of the full-bodied group.

There is some tendency to confuse rum's color with its taste and body, on the assumption that the lighter the color, the lighter the body and the blander the taste. This is only partly true. Color is added after the fact: Both the clean, refined column still rums and the congener-laden pot still rums are clear at distillation.

Light-bodied column still rums that are aged in wood for a time do acquire mellowness along with color, but they simply do not have the potential for developing the kind of fullness and complexity intrinsic to pot still rums. Nevertheless, within a group of rums from a particular area, color will be a clue as to which are more delicate and which are heavier and more redolent. Clear to pale gold signals the former; amber to brown denotes the latter.

97

THE SPIRIT OF '76

There are serious scholars who suggest that rum altered the course of American history. According to one, historian Charles Taussig, Paul Revere embarked on his midnight gallop simply to warn revolutionary leaders Samuel Adams and John Hancock to flee impending arrest—nothing more. En route, the doughty silversmith stopped at the home of Isaac Hall, Captain of the Medford Minute Men and proprietor of a thriving distillery. After a brief respite, and a refreshing draught of Captain Hall's best Old Medford Rum, "He who came a silent horseman, departed a virile and vociferous crusader, with a cry of defiance and not of fear." The aroused Minute Men gathered at Bunker Hill, and the result was the first confrontation of the American Revolutionary War.

Puerto Rican Rums

Puerto Rico, the world's leading rum producer, sets the standard for light-bodied rums, and every aspect of production is geared to achieving clean, muted spirits. Fermentation of the molasses is carefully controlled with the use of special strains of yeast; distillation, of course, is done in column stills.

Three basic rum styles are made in Puerto Rico: *white, gold* or *amber,* and *añejos.* The white rums are the lightest, dryest, and most vodka-like. By law, they are required to come off the still at no less than 180° and can go as high as 189°. They are aged in wood for a minimum of a year, then filtered before bottling to remove any color. White rums are the type most preferred in the U.S., where Puerto Rican rums have captured over 80% of the rum market. As a matter of fact, in 1980, Bacardi rum from Puerto Rico emerged as the most popular brand of spirits in the U.S.

The gold or amber rums are somewhat fuller and a bit more aromatic than the whites. They must be distilled to a minimum of 175° and are aged for a minimum of a year. The most distinctive Puerto Rican rums are the añejos, distilled to the same proof as the golds, but aged from 4 to 6 years, although they may go longer. They are selected for aging potential and are the smoothest and most flavorful of

Puerto Rican rums. While both golds and añejos acquire color from the wood, caramel is usually added before bottling to achieve the desired shade. It may add a trace of flavor.

All Puerto Rican rums are blended after aging, but only with each other, never with neutral grain spirits. Although 80° is standard for Puerto Rican rums, a certain amount of gold is bottled at 151°. This is used for flambé in cooking, and as an ingredient in some exotic drinks.

Myers's has always meant dark, pungent Jamaica rum. But this white rum is distilled in Puerto Rico, a response to the world-wide penchant for lightness.

PUERTO RICAN RUMS BUYING GUIDE

BRANDS ▶

All brands listed below are 80° unless otherwise indicated.

Bacardi: Far and away the leading Puerto Rican rum, and the least rum-like; the white rum (silver label) might pass for vodka in a blind tasting; the gold (amber label) is a bit sweeter and fuller, but it too is quite restrained in taste.

Captain Morgan: A gold, spiced rum.

Don Q.: A little fuller than Bacardi.

Myers's Platinum White and **Myers's Golden Rich:** Both are more robust than most other Puerto Rican rums intended for export, which is not too surprising, since the Myers's label is best known for a full-bodied *Jamaica* rum.

Ron Castillo: Also made by Bacardi; is minimally more rum-like than Bacardi rum itself.

Ron del Barrilito (86°): Something of a savant's favorite in Puerto Rico itself, and not often seen off the island; gold and full-bodied, with pronounced molasses character.

Ronrico: Leans to the opposite end of the Puerto Rican rum spectrum, having faint but recognizable rum character in both white and gold.

Application: White Puerto Rican rums can be used much like vodka—a spirit for all seasons. In addition to use in classic rum drinks such as the Daiquiri, Bacardi (a Daiquiri variation that, by court decree, *must* be made with Bacardi rum), Piña Colada, Rum Punch, and Rum and Cola, white rum is also fine mixed with juices, tonic, or other sodas. Gold rum can be served in the same way, or poured over ice. Añejo is best neat or on the rocks.

How the Daiquiri was Born

The drink known as the Daiquiri could just as easily be called a Rum Sour, because that is essentially what it is. Though Cuban in origin, it was officially christened by a group of American engineers working at the Daiquiri iron mines near Santiago, Cuba, around the turn of the century.

The *yanquis* imbibed the potion, consisting of the light local rum, lime juice, and sugar, for medicinal purposes—or so they alleged. The biggest Daiquiri on record was made in honor of steel magnate Charles Schwab and colleagues when they inspected the Daiquiri mines. Ten bottles of Cuban rum, a pound of sugar, and the juice of 100 limes were poured over ice in a wooden tub and stirred well. As Schwab and his entourage emerged from the pits, each was greeted with a chilled tumbler full of this "medicine." Perhaps the mixture did possess therapeutic properties, since no one in the group came down with a tropical fever.

Jamaica Rums

Production for classic Jamaica rums differs considerably from the Puerto Rican method. The molasses is reinforced with "dunder," skimmings from previous distillations, and fermented with both wild and cultured yeasts. This is followed by double distillation in pot stills, which yields a fairly low proof distillate. The rums are aged for five to eight years, occasionally longer, and after blending are darkened with caramel. These rums are full-bodied and richly aromatic, with an enveloping tang of molasses. Nevertheless, the current vogue for lightness has not gone unnoticed in Jamaica, and today some temperate column still rum is often blended in with the pot still. Proof has been modified, too. At one time, Jamaica rums were bottled at between 86° and 97°; now many are 80°—although 131° and 151° "overproof" rums are also available. And in line with the taste for less hearty spirits, white and gold column still rums are being produced in Jamaica, as well.

 JAMAICA RUMS BUYING GUIDE

BRANDS ▶
Appleton Punch, Lemon Hart, and **Dagger Jamaica:** All examples of dark, pungent Jamaica rums, Lemon Hart may be the fullest.
Appleton's White and **Appleton's Gold:** Contain column still rums; are in the lighter-bodied style; while definitely more flavorful than their Puerto Rican opposite numbers, they are sufficiently muted to represent a departure in Jamaica rums.
Myers's Original Dark Rum: The prototype for deep, intensely flavored Jamaica rums.
London Dock rums are West Indies rums, mainly from Jamaica, that are shipped in bulk to England for aging, blending, and bottling.

Application: The classic Jamaica rums are used in "tropical" drinks—Mai Tai, Zombie, Scorpion, Planter's Punch, etc., and in eggnogs. The white and gold rums are appropriate in the standard light-rum drinks. Aged, opulent Jamaica rums are taken neat, like brandies, or on the rocks.

Rums of Other Countries

Only the major export labels—usually 80°—are described below.

Barbados
Mount Gay: In the middle range—between Puerto Rican and Jamaica rums; amber color; medium body; soft and aromatic, with smoky notes; slightly sweet finish.

Cuba
The prototype for the kind of light rums—white and gold—now made in Puerto Rico, but with slightly more character; understated but definite flavor; not currently exported to the U.S.

Demerara
Named for a river in Guyana, where it is made. **Lemon Hart** (not to be confused with the Jamaican brand) is heavy-bodied; has deep color and aggressive flavor with burnt or smoky undertone. Not as fragrant as Jamaica rums. Also bottled at higher proofs, including 151°.

Haiti
Distilled from fermented sugar cane juice rather than molasses. **Rhum Babancourt** is in the middle range, with a lovely, buoyant quality. The best has a brandy-like style. Babancourt also makes a delightful spiced rum that is worth searching out.

Indonesia:
Batavia Arak is still another type of rum; very dry, light-bodied, and exceedingly fragrant.

Martinique
Pot still rums, made by **Rhum St. James,** are rich and dark, with pronounced rum character—in the heavier middle range. **Rhum Clément** makes slightly lighter but very flavorful column still rums, distilled from fermented cane juice. Martinique rums are popular in France.

South America
Some South American countries produce a rather harsh spirit from sugar cane, called *cachaça,* which is occasionally exported.

Trinidad
Middle-range rums, similar to those from Barbados. **Caroni** rum is typical.

United States
Although now something of a curiosity, a small amount of full-bodied rum is still being made in New England, from West Indies molasses. It is used primarily for industrial purposes.

Virgin Islands
White and gold rums, at the light end of the scale, a shade fuller

than those from Puerto Rico. Exported brands include **Cruzan Rum** and **Ron Carioca.**

British Navy Pusser's Rum (95.5°) is bottled in the British Virgin Islands, but is a blend of Demerara and Trinidad pot still rums. Dark amber; full-bodied, dry and aromatic. This rum was the official daily issue of the British Navy until the practice of rum rations was discontinued in 1970. It has only recently been made available for sale to the general public.

This listing hardly exhausts the sources of rum. Rum is also made in other islands of the West Indies and in Central America, but more for local use than export. Bacardi produces rums in the Puerto Rican style at distilleries in Mexico, South America, Martinique, the Bahamas, and elsewhere.

Rum Clément is one of the few rums made with free-run sugar cane juice rather than molasses. Despite column still distillation, it is a medium-full rum, due to generous time in the cask.

TEQUILA is a spirit made by fermenting and distilling the juice of the blue agave plant, grown in an officially delimited region of west-central Mexico. The area includes the state of Jalisco, parts of adjoining states, and the town of Tequila—for which the spirit is named.

When the Spanish *conquistadores* came to Mexico in the early 1500s, they discovered a native brew that they called *pulque*, a corruption of the Aztec name *octili poliquhqui*. It was a sour, mildly alcoholic beverage fermented from the juice of one of the agaves that grew abundantly in the land. The new arrivals were not impressed with either the flavor or potency of pulque, so they tried distilling it—the first use of the process in the New World. The distilled pulque turned out to be equally unappealing, and the thirsty Spaniards tried again, with other types of agave. They finally found a few whose fermented juice could be distilled into a palatable spirit that they called *mezcal*, after the Aztec word for the agave plant.

In addition to drinking it themselves, the Spanish settlers introduced mezcal to the indigenous population of Mexico. Mezcal had a somewhat checkered history during the period of Spain's occupation of Mexico. In the early days, Spanish mine operators were accused of using it to intoxicate farm workers so that they could be shanghaied for labor in the mines. Public drunkeness, attributed to mezcal, also became a problem from time to time, leading various government bodies to impose periods of prohibition. However, production of mezcal would always be reinstated before very long.

Over a period of time, mezcal from a small region around Tequila—the only place where the blue agave flourished—gained a special reputation for quality. This particular mezcal became known as tequila and, eventually, specific procedures evolved governing its elaboration. Producers have been known to compare tequila to cognac—because its production is confined to a specified geographic area, and because its relationship to mezcal evokes the connection between cognac and brandy. The tequila manufacturers are fond of noting that "all tequila is mezcal, but not all mezcal is tequila."

HOW TEQUILA IS MADE

The blue agave, which once grew wild, is now carefully cultivated to produce the best quality and largest quantity of juice for elaboration into tequila. When the plants reach maturity after 8 to 10 years of growth, the juice-filled cores are harvested. They are called *piñas* (pineapples), which is what they resemble, and can weigh upwards of 100 pounds. After trimming, the *piñas* are halved or quartered, then baked in huge steam ovens until their starch converts to sugar. The cooked *piñas* are shredded and crushed to extract every drop of the sweet juice or *aguamiel* (honey water).

The *aguamiel* is pumped into fermentation tanks and combined with cane sugar and yeast. The addition of sugar is significant, since it can now legally constitute up to 49% of the mixture to be fermented. The more sugar, the less pungent the finished tequila will be, so distillers vary the amount according to the style or market they are seeking. Regulations require that tequila go through a double distillation in pot stills, and be run off at a maximum of 110°. However, it has been suggested that this is honored more in the breach, and that some producers also make partial use of the continuous still.

Most tequila for export is now shipped in bulk and bottled at destination, at 80°. This is in contrast to the 90°, or higher, that was once routine for tequila and that is still true of many tequilas bottled in Mexico.

___ INSIDER'S GUIDE TO TEQUILA ___

Tequila's availability outside of Mexico is fairly recent. Although it was always known in the U.S. along the Mexican border, it was not widely exported until the post-World War II period. By then, travel to Mexico had increased greatly, exposing many more statesiders to this unique spirit. In addition, the major tequila firms pursued an aggressive marketing and advertising policy in the U.S. But the most important factor in the equation was the

MEXICO
Tequila, Mezcal & Pulque Regions

USA

PACIFIC
OCEAN

GULF OF
MEXICO

• Torreón
• Durango
San Luis Potosí
Tequila • Tepatitlán
Guadalajara
Manzanillo
MEXICO
CITY
Tuxtla
Gutiérrez
Acapulco
Oaxaca

Yucatán Peninsula

☐ TEQUILA
▨ MEZCAL
☐ PULQUE

Tequila, mezcal, and pulque are all derived from the agave plant,
which is not a cactus. But tequila may only be produced from a
specified variety—the blue Agave Tequiliana Weber—and only if it
comes from the delimited zone circling the town of Tequila.

change in the nature of the product itself. In recent years, variations in formula (such as the increased use of cane sugar in the *aguamiel*) and refinement of distillation practices have resulted in a product—for export, at least—that is less assertive and more mixable. All these elements have contributed to tequila's acceptance in the U.S.

With the changes in process and lower proof at bottling, some critics claim that tequila is being "vodkaized." Not quite. Present-day tequila still displays a peppery, green plant taste and aroma, but it is a far cry from the rank, harsh, vegetal spirit it was.

Tequila is available in three styles: *white* or *silver, gold,* and *añejo*. All are not necessarily offered by every producer. White or silver tequila is colorless and bottled with little or no aging, which makes it a touch harsh. Gold tequila gets some time in used barrels, which both softens and tints it a bit, although the pale, straw-gold color probably owes more to the addition of caramel. *Añejo*, or aged, tequila is required to have at least a year in wood, but in practice gets at least 3 years. It is smoother and mellower than either white or gold.

Tequila labels usually bear the letters "DGN" or "NOM" as a quality seal. These are the initials of Mexican government bureaus concerned with standards.

TEQUILA MYTHS

Despite its new-found popularity, tequila is still surrounded by a host of myths and misconceptions—possibly because it was developed in a country that has a somewhat exotic and mysterious history. Even today, you are apt to hear that tequila is "bottled lightning"—so potent that if you drink water the morning after you have freely imbibed it, you will revive its effect and become drunk again. A baseless tale, of course.

But the wildest tequila legend of all—that it is hallucinogenic—springs from something quite innocent, a confusion in spelling. As noted in the text, the Aztecs called the agave plant *mezcal*—which North Americans frequently misspell *mescal.* It happens that there is a cactus called *mescal* in Mexico, the source of the hallucinogen mescaline. The spelling mix-up has led some otherwise accurate writers to report that tequila comes from the same plant as mescaline, and is therefore capable of inducing a hallucinogenic experience. This story, which had particular currency in the 1960s, still crops up, attested to by gullible souls who are convinced tequila lifted them to a higher plane.

BRANDS ▶

All those listed are 80° unless otherwise noted.

Jose Cuervo: By far the leading brand in the U.S.; a muted, peppery, bittersweet style characteristic of most exported tequilas.

Cuervo 1800: An añejo, rounder than the white or gold.

Herradura (92°): Bottled in Mexico; the label states, "Distilled from 100% blue agave"; definitely pungent tequila taste; smooth and clean with no rankness; in all three styles.

Sauza's Conmemorativo: Similar to but dryer than Cuervo 1800.

Montezuma, Pepe Lopez, Sauza: Similar, differing from each other only in small particulars; they generally conform to the basic description for the category.

Small local brands abound in the southwest and southern California; these are sometimes bottled at above 80°, and are not as clean as the national brands.

Application: Traditionally, tequila is taken neat, preceded by a lick of salt and followed by a bite into a lime wedge. This procedure is called *Los Tres Cuates*—The Three Chums. Alternatively, neat tequila can be followed by a chaser of Sangrita, a well-seasoned tomato and orange juice mixture. The most popular tequila cocktails are the Margarita, Sunrise, and Tequila Sour. It can also be combined with tomato or fruit juices, with carbonated mixers, or with dry vermouth for a sort of Martini. Añejo tequila is usually poured over ice.

Other Agave Beverages

Almendrado

Also called *creme de tequila,* it is a sweet, milky, almond-flavored beverage made on a tequila base. It is actually a tequila liqueur and long preceded amaretto, which it somewhat resembles.

Mezcal

This continues to be made in various parts of Mexico: in an area north and east of the delimited tequila region, along the southwest coastal area, and down in the southern tip of the country. Mezcal is distilled from several varieties of agave, but is not subject to the same quality standards as tequila. Mezcal is sometimes bottled with an agave worm (*con gusano*), a creature that, when alive, makes its home inside the plant. Like many other bizarre items of food or drink, the worm has an unsubstantiated reputation as an aphrodisiac. Very little mezcal, with or without worm, is found beyond Mexico's borders.

THE BLUE AGAVE

The official botanical designation for the blue agave is *Agave tequilana weber*—Weber being the botanist who identified it as a distincitive species. There are, as a matter of fact, about 400 types of agave, several of which are used in Mexico for alcoholic beverages other than tequila. Agaves as a group are also referred to as *magueys*—the name given them by Spanish explorers in Mexico, or as *mezcals*—the Aztec term. By whatever name, agaves are members of the *Amaryllidaceae* family. They are *not* part of the cactus family—a common misconception.

Liqueurs

LIQUEURS (or cordials: The terms mean the same) are flavored, sweetened spirits. The term "liqueur" is based on the Latin *liquifacere,* meaning to dissolve, and refers to the flavorings dissolved in the spirits. "Cordial" stems from *cordialis,* Latin for pertaining to the heart, since early examples of these potions were prescribed to stimulate the circulatory system. "Cordial" is more common in the U.S., possibly a legacy from the Puritans who did not mind a nip now and then but were put off by the naughty French sound of "liqueur."

By whatever name, cordial these spirits are. U.S. government regulations require that they have a minimum of 2½% sugar content, and most contain considerably more. In fact, liqueurs with up to 10% sugar may be labelled "dry." They come in a range of hues, and they are imbued with the vivid flavors of fruits, herbs, spices, flowers, seeds, roots, mint, chocolate, coffee, and nuts—to name only the most common. Many are fairly low in alcohol—60° or less—but even the more potent are smooth and unctuous, delightfully easy to sip. They can be made anywhere that spirits are distilled and their variety is formidable.

Anyone familiar with today's enticing liqueurs would be dismayed, even bewildered, by the initial attempts. Early liqueurs were foul-tasting mixtures, brewed as elixirs to prolong life, induce love, and accomplish any number of other worthy goals. The medieval alchemists and apothecaries who experimented with *aqua vitae* were often herbalists as well, familiar with the medicinal—and allegedly magical—properties of many plants. So it seemed sensible to them to add botanicals to spirits, in hopes of enhancing their therapeutic and supernatural properties. Much of this took place in monasteries, since the friars had the education, time, and resources for such activities.

This venerable complex is The Abbey at Fécamp, France. It is the home of Bénédictine liqueur.

In an effort to make the nostrums more palatable, some were sweetened with honey; not surprisingly, they became the most popular. However, the flowering of liqueurs as we know them today was essentially a by-product of the 16th- and 17th-century explorations that brought cane sugar, new fruits, and aromatic plants to Europe from across the sea. Given this wealth of exotic ingredients, mixologists of the era applied their knowledge of distillation and flavor extraction, eventually coming up with an assortment of sweet, fragrant spirits that were bewitching in taste if not in effect.

The fame of these delightful new beverages spread across Europe. Catherine de Medici, often credited with introducing *haute cuisine* to the French, is said to have included liqueurs among the gastronomic novelties she brought with her to France from Italy as a royal bride in

1533. Perhaps she helped popularize liqueurs, but they were not totally unknown in her new country. By the time Catherine arrived, at least one monastery in France—the Bénédictine Abbey of Fécamp—was already producing a liqueur whose name is famous to this day.

Some of the early names in commercial production of liqueurs have survived as well. The house of Bols was founded in Holland in 1575; a few years later, a German company called Der Lachs launched Danziger Goldwasser, a citrus-and-spice-flavored cordial flecked with gold leaf particles. The presence of gold, of course, reflected the association of liqueurs with alchemists, whose passion for the precious metal was partially dictated by their faith in its curative powers. Eighteenth-century arrivals on the liqueur scene included the Dutch firm DeKuyper and the French Rocher Frères and Marie Brizard. A big spurt in liqueur production was fostered by the invention of the continuous still in the 19th century. The ready availability of inexpensive, neutral spirits that could be used as a base for all manner of flavorings encouraged the development of many liqueurs. This was the period that spawned or advanced the great standard flavors—crème de cacao, crème de menthe, apricot, and other fruits, and such classics as Cointreau, Grand Marnier, Chartreuse, and Bénédictine. Nothing very interesting happened to liqueurs in the intervening years—until a decade ago, when young people searching for fresh taste experiences rediscovered the sensual, flavorful properties of liqueurs. This display of interest triggered an avalanche of new liqueur types and flavors, which in turn has made these liquid confections the most exciting group in the spirit realm.

THE POUSSE CAFÉ

Also known as the bartender's bane, the Pousse Café is a dazzling, radiant drink—and one of the most difficult to prepare. The name translates as "push down the coffee," reflecting the potion's status as an after-dinner *digestif*. The Pousse is composed by pouring liqueurs of different hues into a tall, narrow liqueur glass, one at a time. If properly executed, the liqueurs will remain separate, in multicolored layers, giving a rainbow effect. It requires a steady hand and—more important—a knowledge of the specific gravity of each liqueur, since they must be poured in descending order of weight. There is no absolute guideline, since one brand's triple sec may well vary from another's in density and weight. But there is one quite dependable combination: *crème de cassis* (reddish-purple) as the bottom layer, Chartreuse (green) in the middle, and California brandy (amber) on top. To assemble, pour the *crème de cassis* in without splashing the sides of the glass. To layer the green Chartreuse, place the tip of a demitasse spoon in the glass, just above the level of the *cassis* layer, bowl down. Pour the measured quantity of Chartreuse slowly over the back of the spoon. Repeat with the brandy—or, if you prefer, substitute an *eau de vie*. Some bartenders are so skillful that they can arrange seven or eight layers in a glass. This is known as the "Judy Garland," or over-the-rainbow, version.

How Liqueurs Are Made

All liqueurs start with a base of spirits—more often than not, neutral grain alcohol, although any spirit may be used. The flavor of a liqueur may be imparted in a variety of ways.

Distillation:

The flavoring substances are combined with the base spirit and then distilled in a pot still to extract and concentrate the flavors. This method is used particularly with seeds, such as anise and caraway, and for dried peels. Delicate flavorings, such as mint or flowers, are sometimes distilled in water rather than alcohol, and then redistilled to further concentrate the essential flavoring oils.

Maceration:

The flavoring substance is steeped in the base spirit and agitated until it yields its flavor, aroma, and color. The liquid is separated from the solids by filtration or centrifuging. The leftover solids may then be distilled to extract the last bit of flavor, as well as any remaining alcohol. Maceration is used mainly with soft fruits such as berries.

Percolation:

This is basically the same process as that used to brew coffee: The spirit is pumped over the flavoring material again and again until the flavor has been extracted. Here, too, the flavoring agent may be distilled after it has been separated from the liquid. Percolation is used with such flavorings as cocoa beans or vanilla pods.

Cordial makers do not necessarily handle their own flavor extraction. Natural essences and extracts are available from huge international flavor houses, which scour the globe for their esoteric raw materials—and sell to all comers. This suggests that producers draw from the same sources for a good proportion of their flavoring material.

One of the relatively new liqueurs, distinguished by the subtle taste of hazelnuts. A product of Italy.

Artificial flavors are frowned upon and their use is strictly regulated in almost every country. In the U.S., any domestically made product containing synthetic flavoring above one thousand parts per million must be labeled "artificial" or "imitation." The French are more diplomatic; an artificially flavored liqueur bears the word *fantaisie* on its label.

The preparation of a liqueur is far more complex than simple flavor extraction. Every liqueur is a blend to some extent; even when a single flavor predominates, it is almost always accented by judicious additions of other extracts. A little vanilla is invariably added to crème de cacao to heighten the perception of chocolate, chocolate may be added to apricot, and anise is emphasized by orange- and lemon-peel distillates. In the case of an herbal liqueur, dozens of individual flavors may be combined.

After the flavor is set, the liqueur is sweetened (usually with sugar syrup), the alcohol reduced with water to the desired proof, and natural food color added if necessary. Liqueurs are not usually aged for any great length of time, but often there is a short "resting" period between the different stages of preparation and before bottling.

INSIDER'S GUIDE TO LIQUEURS

Liqueurs can be divided into groups by many different systems but they are most easily categorized according to flavor type or essential style feature. The major groupings are:

- fruit flavors
- seed, nut, and other individual plant flavors
- botanical mixtures: herbs, spices, plants
- liquor-based liqueurs
- cream liqueurs

There is a fair amount of overlapping, since many liqueurs are quite complicated and do not readily lend themselves to neat classification. Beyond that, liqueurs are divided into *generics* and *proprietaries.* Generics are liqueurs of a particular type that can be made by any manufacturer and bottled under a company name. Crème de menthe and anisette are examples of generics. Proprietaries are liqueurs known by a registered name and made according to a specific formula: Examples are **Chartreuse, Grand Marnier,** or **Bénédictine.** A number come packed in handsome and sometimes unique decanter bottles.

Unlike the proprietaries, generics don't run that much of a range in style and quality. The leading producers in both Europe and the U.S. are generally dependable, although there are differences. Painting with a broad brush, one might characterize European liqueurs as more delicate and complex, and the U.S. product as more intense and forthright—you know what you are tasting. European liqueur makers have a nice way with cherry, raspberry, strawberry, amaretto, sambuca, and kümmel. U.S. producers get good results with sloe gin, peppermint schnapps, crème de menthe, blackberry, banana, anisette, and chocolate combinations.

Issues of leading U.S. firms are, as a rule, agreeable, and similar in quality, but exhibit stylistic differences. **Arrow** tends to be quite sweet and a bit heavy; **DeKuyper's** sweetness is moderated and the flavors are a bit more subtle; **Leroux** and **Hiram Walker** are in the middle ground.

European liqueurs are quite pricey in the U.S. market—sometimes more than double the domestic version. It should be noted that a number of European firms such as **Bols** and **DeKuyper** (Holland), **Garnier** (France), and perhaps others, also manufacture liqueurs in the U.S. under the same brand name.

Fruit Flavors

This group of liqueurs has proliferated over the years, and now includes all manner of fruits—even a kiwi in Australia. In order to evoke the luscious taste and aroma of fresh, ripe fruit, liqueur makers and flavor houses employ a variety of techniques to extract the maximum flavor the fruit can offer. Sometimes the whole fruit is used—even the kernels inside the pits, as in the case of apricots. Sometimes only a part is used, as with citrus liqueurs, which derive much of their flavor from peels. As previously indicated, whispers of complementary flavorings may be added to enhance the impact of the fruit. As a category, fruits are the most delicate and difficult liqueurs to make—and they decline with time.

Some fruit liqueurs are called "brandies" in Europe, creating a confusion with the true fruit *eaux de vie* such as kirsch or framboise. Once you become aware of their existence, however, these "brandies" should not be difficult to recognize. They are almost always color-cued to the raw fruit—gold for apricot, red for cherry, purplish for blackberry, etc.—and are lower in alcohol content than the true *eaux de vie.*

In the U.S., fruit-flavored brandies (peach-flavored brandy, blackberry-flavored brandy, etc.) are a sub-group of fruit liqueurs; they must be made on a brandy base and be at least 70°. They are somewhat dryer and lighter in body than other fruit liqueurs. On the other hand, fruit liqueurs labeled crème (as in crème de cassis) have a soft, smooth, almost syrupy consistency. Crèmes have the sweetest taste among fruit liqueurs, and are fairly low in alcohol.

FRUIT-FLAVORED LIQUEURS
BUYING GUIDE

In the chart that follows, "G" indicates generic, "P" indicates proprietary.
Agreeable brands of generics are listed after the descriptions.

FLAVOR SOURCE	DESCRIPTION
Apple	Straightforward, uncomplicated apple flavor; modestly alcoholic. Ⓟ **Berentzen Appel** *(Germany)* Ⓟ **Schnapple** *(Germany)*
Apricot	Ⓖ Made as liqueur and as flavored brandy. Both display fresh apricot aroma, with an undertone of bitter almond flavor from the kernel. (U.S.: **Leroux, DeKuyper, Hiram Walker**)
	Ⓟ **Garnier Abricotine** *(France):* Noted for pronounced apricot flavor, medium body, and sweetness. Ⓟ **Marie Brizard Apry** *(France):* Has complexity and interest due to the addition of small amounts of other fruits, but has less apricot flavor.
Banana	Ⓖ Whether labeled banana liqueur or crème de banane, it is sweet and heavy-bodied, with intense and sometimes overpowering banana flavor. Poor examples smell like furniture polish. (U.S.: **Leroux** is pleasant)
	Ⓟ **Pisang Ambon** *(Holland):* Pronounced banana flavor with hints of other tropical fruits and citrus. Exotic quality.
Blackberry	Ⓖ Made as liqueur and as flavored brandy. Both have deep, purplish-amber color, fragrant blackberry aroma and flavor. Blackberry-flavored brandy is one of the traditional fruit liqueurs to which devotees ascribe medicinal properties. (U.S.: **Leroux, Arrow**)
Cassis (black currant)	Ⓖ Crème de cassis is reddish-purple, sweet, and syrupy, with a rich currant taste. Made-in-U.S. versions are berryish. Usually 40° or lower. Should be purchased fresh and used in a reasonable time or it will oxidize; browning signals

FLAVOR SOURCE	DESCRIPTION
(black currant) cont'd	oxidation. (The best examples still come from the area where the liqueur originated, around Dijon in the Burgundy region of France. **L'Héritier-Guyot** and **Ropiteau Frères** are among the finest.)
Cherry	Ⓖ Made as liqueur and as flavored brandy. Liqueur is bright red, with modest cherry flavor. American cherry-flavored brandies and European "cherry brandies" are not as sweet, have less color, and truer flavor. **Cherry Rocher** *(France),* sometimes referred to as "cherry brandy," is fairly light in body, color, and sweetness but with distinct cherry flavor and almond undertone. Fairly typical of other French cherry liqueurs, which also include **Marie Brizard, Garnier,** and **Cusenier.**
	Ⓖ **Maraschino** is a distinctive cherry liqueur made from marasca cherries grown in northeastern Italy and Yugoslavia. Made by a unique process, it combines a distillate of the pits and the pomace left from making cherry wine. Clear color and sweet, intense cherry-almond flavor. *(Italy:* **Stock***)*
	Ⓟ **Peter Heering** *(Denmark):* Known as Cherry Heering in Europe, it is dark red with complex cherry flavor; winey and dry for a liqueur. Possibly the most famous cherry liqueur in the world. Ⓟ **Cherry Marnier** *(France):* Has unmistakable pit (almond) accents. Ⓟ **Cherristock** *(Italy):* Made primarily from marasca cherries but unlike maraschino. Medium body with good cherry flavor, moderately sweet. Ⓟ **Grant's Morella Cherry Brandy** *(U.K.):* Made with morella cherries from Kent, on a brandy base. Light brownish-red, good cherry flavor, reasonably dry.
Cranberry	Ⓟ **Boggs Cranberry Liqueur** *(U.S.):* Bright red with delightful tart-sweet cranberry flavor and a touch of astringency.

FLAVOR SOURCE	DESCRIPTION
	Ⓟ **Regnier's Cranberria** *(U.S.):* Sweet and less distinctively cranberry.
Lime	Ⓟ **Cusenier Freezolime** *(France):* Light green with pungent lime-peel fragrance and taste. Syrupy body, fairly sweet; 80°.
Melon	Ⓟ **Midori Melon Liqueur** *(Japan):* Light green with a pleasing melony flavor. It is perceived as honeydew because of the color. (Although the Japanese created this category, several American melon liqueurs are now available, but have little distinction.)
Orange	There are two basic types of generic orange liqueurs, each with its own style: Ⓖ **Curaçao:** First developed by the Dutch; flavored with peel of bitter oranges from the West Indian island of the same name. Most curaçao is an orangey-amber color, but some is available in other shades, including blue. (U.S.: **Hiram Walker, Leroux, Bols**) Ⓖ **Triple Sec:** Made from both bitter and sweet orange peels. It is thicker, sweeter, more delicate in flavor, and higher in alcohol than curaçao; colorless. (U.S.: **Arrow, Leroux**)
	Ⓟ **Cointreau** *(France):* Essentially a triple sec of high quality, it has intense orange flavor and aroma; medium-bodied, quite sweet; 80°. Ⓟ **Grand Marnier** *(France):* Made on a base of cognac and flavored with bitter orange peel; the cognac adds complexity to the moderate orange flavor; amber color; 80°. **Grand Marnier Cuvée Spéciale,** produced to commemorate the company's 150th anniversary, is made with all *Fine Champagne* cognac. It is fuller and richer than the standard bottlings and somewhat dryer. Other French orange liqueurs based on cognac include **Cognac à l'Orange** and **Sablorange.** Ⓟ **Aurum** *(Italy):* Based on Italian brandy; has an exquisite fresh orange flavor; one of the best of this genre.

FLAVOR SOURCE	DESCRIPTION
Peach	Ⓖ Made as liqueur and as flavored brandy. Peach flavor and aroma in both are rather muted. One of the less successful fruit liqueurs. (U.S.: **Hiram Walker, DeKuyper**)
Pear	Ⓖ Like *eau de vie de poire,* pear liqueurs have intense fresh pear fragrance but somewhat more modest pear flavor. **Dettling** *(Switzerland)* and **Jean Danflou** *(France)* are particularly luscious examples; **Zwack** *(Austria)* is admirable, and **Marie Brizard** *(France)* is quite appealing.
Plum	Ⓟ **Aki** *(Japan):* One of the few examples of plum liqueur now available; sweet and red, it also tastes red—vaguely cherryish-berryish.
Raspberry	Ⓖ The few U.S.-produced raspberry liqueurs and flavored brandies just don't make it. (French raspberry liqueurs such as **Marie Brizard Raspberry de Bourdeaux,** and those from **Jean Danflou,** and **Trenel** are inviting.)
	Ⓟ **Chambord Royale** *(France):* Black raspberry color and a berryish aroma and taste that do not, however, precisely evoke raspberry; syrupy and sweet, with a hint of chocolate in the aftertaste; low proof—33°.
Sloeberry	Ⓖ **Sloe gin:** The sloeberry, botanically a plum, is used with cherry and other flavors in making this bright-red liqueur, with its cherryish taste. At one time, the spirit base was gin, but neutral spirits are frequently used now; a compensating touch of juniper flavor may be added. (U.S.: **Leroux, Arrow, Mr. Boston**)
	Ⓖ **Prunelle:** Also made from the sloeberry, but seldom seen.
Strawberry	Ⓖ Another fruit that U.S. producers have not yet captured. Most examples, although made with natural flavors, have a synthetic, candyish taste. **(DeKuyper, Hiram Walker, Arrow)**

FLAVOR SOURCE	DESCRIPTION
	A blend of European *fraises des bois* (wild strawberries) yields a more fragrant, truer strawberry character than the cultivated variety. (France: **Dolfi**)
Tangerine	Ⓟ **Mandarine Napoléon** *(Belgium):* Made on a cognac base with a tangerine-citrus-brandy flavor; candyish but appealing; 80°. The same product, when made in the cognac region of France, is called **Mandarine Impériale.** Ⓟ **Van der Hum** *(South Africa):* Made with *naartjies,* a local tangerine, on a brandy base. Van der Hum translates as "what's his name"—presumably in honor of the originator, whose name has been forgotten.

This label denotes a commemorative bottling, marking the 150th anniversary of Grand Marnier. It is richer, dryer, and more complex than the standard Grand Marnier, and comes in a hand-decorated decanter bottle.

123

Botanical Mixture: Herbs, Spices, Plants

The first liqueurs ever made were of this type—particularly those developed by monks for medicinal purposes. For this, the group is sometimes referred to as "monastery" liqueurs. They are flavored with combinations of aromatics, including angelica, gentian and ginger roots, anise seeds, cloves, cinnamon, nutmeg, sage, rosemary, thyme, fennel, juniper, lavender, vanilla pods—a veritable botanical garden. No single flavor predominates in these liqueurs and the overall impression is fragrant and pungent, although each example is distinct and individual within itself. "Monastery" liqueurs tend to be fairly potent; those listed here are about 80° unless otherwise noted.

 ★   **BOTANICAL LIQUEURS BUYING GUIDE**   ★

The following liqueurs are all proprietaries, except as noted.

BRANDS ▶

Abtei *(Israel):* Herbal flavors on a brandy base.

Ambrosia *(Canada):* More caramel flavor than herbal.

Averna *(Italy):* Herbal mixture; semi-sweet, with bitter undertone; 68°.

Bénédictine *(France):* Made by what is alleged to be the oldest existing recipe for any liqueur, with over 20 herbs and other plants in its blend; aromatic, sweet, and full-bodied; dark amber color.

B & B *(France):* A 20th-century offshoot of Bénédictine, made to accommodate the taste for drier beverages. It combines about 60% Bénédictine and 40% cognac, which substantially cuts the level of sweetness.

Brontë *(U.K.):* Produced in Yorkshire, home of the famous Brontë sisters; spicy, fruity flavor; medium sweet.

Chartreuse *(France):* The formula for this liqueur still remains the property of the Carthusian monastery that has been producing it, on and off, for more than 300 years.

Made with 130 herbs, in several styles. Green-label Chartreuse is 110°, green in color, quite dry with a pungent herby taste; yellow-label Chartreuse is 86°, yellow in color, sweeter than the green, softer and less assertive. **Chartreuse VEP,** 108°, and aged for 12 years or more, displays a mellow roundness. It is quite rare, as is the **Elixir Végétal de la Grande Chartreuse,** 142°, which is generally used for medicinal purposes.

Claristine *(U.S.):* Made according to a formula purchased from the Claristine Nuns of Dirant, Belgium; herby-spicy, honeyish taste.

Cordial Médoc *(France):* Made from a mixture of fruits accented with herbs and chocolate, on a brandy base; subtle, complex flavor; moderately sweet.

Cuarenta y Tres *(Spain):* The name means "43," presumably the number of herbs and other plants in the flavoring blend; outstanding notes are vanilla and a touch of citrus; quite sweet and syrupy.

Elixir D'Anvers *(Belgium):* Herby-spicy, with noticeable cinnamon accent; moderately sweet.

Escorial Green *(Germany):* The green hue and herby character evoke Chartreuse; 112°.

Fior de Alpe *(Italy):* Herby flavor; small twigs are placed inside bottle, around which some of the sugar in the liqueur crystallizes.

Galliano *(Italy):* Herb-seed flavorings; noticeable vanilla plus a hint of anise; syrupy, moderately sweet; popular in the U.S. as a cocktail ingredient, it has inspired similar products such as **Liquore Roiano** and **Valentino,** which are not up to its quality.

Goldwasser *(Germany):* Now a generic made by a number of German liqueur producers, although the prototype, **Der Lachs Danziger Goldwasser,** is still being produced. Citrus-caraway flavor, but the distinguishing characteristic is floating particles of gold leaf.

Izarra *(France):* Like Chartreuse, this liqueur is made green, at 100°, and yellow, at 80°; both are similar to Chartreuse, though not quite as distinctive or defined.

Jägermeister *(Germany):* Over 50 herbs and other plants contribute the forthright, pungent herb flavor; definite bitter undertone.

Nassau Royale *(Bahamas):* Herby-spicy with noticeable vanilla; sweet; medium-light body.

Strega *(Italy):* Over 70 herbs and other botanicals in the blend; pungent flavor with citrus note; quite aggressive.

Trappistine *(France):* Herbal flavor on a base of armagnac.

Tuaca *(Italy):* Vanilla dominates the flavor mix, supplemented with herbs and other botanicals; medium body; smooth, sweet.

Vieille Curé *(France):* Another herbal blend available in green, 100° and yellow 86°; green has more definite flavor and is a bit drier than yellow; unusual "stained glass" bottle.

Seed, Nut, and Other Individual Plant Flavors

This category covers liqueurs derived from seeds, nuts, or other plants in which a single flavor predominates. Chocolate, mint, and anise flavored liqueurs are all part of this group. Liqueurs labeled "crème" *(crème de cacao, crème de menthe)* are particularly sweet, velvety, and low in alcohol.

★ **LIQUEURS BUYING GUIDE** ★

In the chart that follows, "G" indicates generic, "P" indicates proprietary. Agreeable brands of generics are listed after the descriptions

FLAVOR SOURCE	DESCRIPTION
Anise Seed	Ⓖ *Anisette:* A sweet, aromatic, low-proof liqueur with a licorice-like flavor derived from anise seed—one of the oldest and most widely used flavorings in the liqueur maker's repertoire. Anisette includes small amounts of other flavorings, particularly citrus peels, which add depth to the finished product. Usually colorless, but occasionally tinted bright red. U.S. anisettes are cleaner and less complex than European. (U.S.: **Arrow, Leroux, Hiram Walker;** France: **Marie Brizard,** Italy: **Stock**)

FLAVOR SOURCE	DESCRIPTION
	Anise aperitifs: A group of liqueurs with a licorice-like flavor, made with anise seed and other herbs, they are dryer than anisettes and more alcoholic—mostly in the 90° range. Found in all the Mediterranean countries, where they are usually taken with water, which turns them an opalescent yellowish-white. They include the following: Ⓖ **Pastis** *(France):* Made by macerating anise and other flavors in alcohol; 90°. One of the replacements for the notorious absinthe, banned as lethal over half a century ago because its flavorings included wormwood, an allegedly poisonous plant, and perhaps because it was over 120°. Ⓖ **Ouzo** and **Mastic** *(Greece):* Ouzo is the dryer. Ⓖ **Anesone** *(Italy):* Also made in the U.S. by Leroux. Ⓖ **Ojen** and **Chinchon** *(Spain)* Ⓖ **Raki** *(Turkey and the Middle East)* Ⓟ **Pernod** *(France):* Originally a brand of absinthe, but made to a new formulation after the ban. Not a *pastis,* since its flavor comes from a distillation rather than a maceration of the anise seed and other botanicals; 86°. Ⓟ **Ricard** *(France):* A *pastis;* the company that produces this brand is now also making **Pacific,** a non-alcoholic *pastis,* by macerating the flavorings in water. Ⓟ **Herbsaint** *(U.S.):* Made in New Orleans, which boasts a large population of French heritage.
Caraway Seed	Ⓖ **Kümmel:** One of the oldest liqueurs. Originated in Holland in the 16th century, but later was made throughout northern Europe. Caraway (as in rye bread) is the essential flavor, but it also includes cumin seed and an undertone of anise. Fairly dry, colorless, and usually 70° or over. The type called *allasch* kümmel, made in Germany, is considered to be of extra-high quality, albeit on the sweet side. (U.S.: **De-Kuyper;** Germany: **Gilka;** Holland: **Bols**)
Chocolate	Ⓖ **Crème de cacao:** The basic chocolate liqueur, made by every liqueur house;

FLAVOR SOURCE	DESCRIPTION
Chocolate (cont'd)	always has an accent of vanilla; wide variation in depth of chocolate flavor from brand to brand, but U.S. examples tend to be more chocolatey and a bit less sweet than European. Made both brown and colorless; the latter has lighter chocolate flavor. (U.S.: **Arrow, Leroux, Hiram Walker;** France: **Rocher, Marie Brizard**)
	Ⓖ **Chocolate combinations:** Chocolate's agreeable nature is reflected in the number of liqueurs in which it is combined with other flavors. **Royal** *(France)* and **Hiram Walker** (U.S.) offer an extensive line of liqueurs in which chocolate is mated with mint, coffee, almond, or fruits.
	Ⓟ **Droste Bittersweet Chocolate Liqueur** *(Holland):* More sweet than bitter, with true chocolate bar flavor; golden brown. Ⓟ **Marmot Chocolate Liqueur** *(Switzerland):* Distinguished by the bits of solid chocolate afloat in it. Ⓟ **Rathaus Swiss Chocolate Liqueur** *(Switzerland):* Rich chocolate taste; dark brown color. Ⓟ **Cheri-Suisse** *(Switzerland):* Chocolate-cherry combination, reminiscent of a chocolate-covered cherry; unfortunately, the cherry adds a medicinal overtone. Ⓟ **Choclair** *(U.S.):* Chocolate-coconut combination; tastes like a liquid Mounds candy bar. Other examples of this flavor mix are **Afrikoko** *(Africa)* and **Chococo** *(Virgin Islands).* Ⓟ **Sabra** *(Israel):* Chocolate-orange, in which the orange predominates; pleasing flavor overall. Ⓟ **Vandermint** *(Holland):* Chocolate-mint combination; reasonably well-balanced, although the mint is the stronger note. Ⓟ **Veraña** *(Spain):* Chocolate-citrus, plus other flavorings that add depth and complexity.
Coconut	A fairly new flavor on the liqueur scene. Made on a rum base, and offering light but true coconut character.

FLAVOR SOURCE	DESCRIPTION
	℗ **CocoRibe** *(U.S.):* Made with Virgin Islands rum. ℗ **Ron Coco** *(Puerto Rico):* Made with Puerto Rican rum.
Coffee	Ⓖ **Crème de cafe, crème de mocha, coffee liqueur:** Names given to the sweeter, lower-proof examples. Ⓖ **Coffee-flavored brandy:** Made by some U.S. liqueur firms; is dryer, 70°; made on a brandy base. Regardless of type, the sweetness of any coffee liqueur is moderated by the bitter undertone of the coffee itself. Styles vary widely depending on the source of the coffee and the accent flavorings. (U.S.: **Arrow, Leroux;** France: **Marie Brizard;** Italy: **Stock**)
	℗ **Kahlua** *(Mexico):* The one that started the vogue for coffee liqueurs; good coffee flavor; hint of molasses adds smoothness. ℗ **Tia Maria** *(Jamaica):* Rich coffee flavor, subtle and complex; drier and lighter-bodied than the average coffee liqueur. ℗ **Chase & Sanborn Coffee Liqueur** *(U.S.):* A famous coffee brand name now associated with a distinctive espresso-flavored liqueur. ℗ **Gallwey's Irish Coffee Liqueur** *(Ireland):* Based on Irish whiskey; rich coffee flavor accented by honey and herbs. ℗ **Caffe Lolita** *(U.S.):* Smooth flavor; in the Kahlua style.
Elder Bush	Ⓖ **Sambuca:** Licorice flavor from the fruit of the elder bush. This colorless liqueur is sweet, velvety, intensely flavored, and often quite alcoholic—80° or higher. (U.S.: **Bucca di Amore;** Italy: **Sambuca Romana**—probably the best-known; **Galliano, Molinari, Patrician Sarti**)
Fruit Pit Kernels and Nuts	The bitter almond character of apricot, peach, cherry, and other fruit pit kernels has made them an important flavor source for many liqueurs. They are used as an accent in nut-flavored liqueurs and also, as noted, in a number of fruit liqueurs. Ⓖ **Amaretto** liqueur is based on apricot

FLAVOR SOURCE	DESCRIPTION
Fruit Pit Kernels and Nuts (cont'd)	kernels, enhanced with vanilla, vanillin, and other flavorings. The essential flavor is bitter almond, with hints of fruit and vanilla. Amarettos are sweet with a somewhat syrupy body. The type originated in Italy, but is now being widely made in the U.S. with varying degrees of success. (Italy: **Amaretto di Saronno** was the first, and remains the standard; **Amaretto di Torino** is pleasantly full-bodied.)
	ⓖ **Amaretto combinations:** A number of U.S. liqueur firms have combined amaretto with compatible flavors—chocolate, coffee, coconut, strawberry; some have combined it with brandy, to cut the sweetness. (U.S.: **Leroux, DeKuyper, Regnier, Garnier, Hiram Walker**)
	ⓖ **Crème de noyaux** or **crème de almond:** Flavored with almond and fruit pit kernels; sweet, velvety; usually tinted a light, bright red.
	ⓟ **Frangelico** *(Italy):* Hazelnuts are the informing flavor, pleasantly modified by bitter almond accents and what seems to be a hint of chocolate. ⓟ **Pistasha** *(U.S.):* A green, sweet, nut-flavored liqueur with a light note of pistachio in the aftertaste. ⓟ **Praline** *(U.S.):* Almost as sweet as the confection for which it is named, with a little pecan and vanilla flavor hovering around the edges. ⓟ **Walneta** *(Italy):* Identifiable walnut taste in this sweet, fragrant liqueur.
Mint	ⓖ **Crème de menthe:** One of the great classic liqueurs. Offers an essentially straightforward peppermint flavor, although there are variations in sharpness from brand to brand. European brands tend to be rounder and less intense than the American. Green is the most common color, but *crème de menthe* is also made colorless, gold, and occasionally red. (U.S.: **Arrow, DeKuyper, Leroux, Paramount;** France: **Marie Brizard, Freezomint**)

FLAVOR SOURCE	DESCRIPTION
	ⓖ **Peppermint schnapps:** Drier, less syrupy, and higher proof than *crème de menthe;* usually colorless. Its recent surge in popularity has led to the introduction of *spearmint schnapps.* (U.S.: **Arrow, DeKuyper**)
	ⓟ **Get Pippermint** *(France):* Has much more intense mint taste than most mint liqueurs, which balances the sweetness and imparts an almost menthol quality. ⓟ **Rumple Minze** *(Germany):* Sharp, clean mint taste; 100°. ⓟ **Steel** (U.S.): Sharp peppermint schnapps; 85°.
Spices— assorted	Spices are generally an accent but there are a few liqueurs distinguished by the dominance of a single spice flavor. ⓖ **Cinnamon Schnapps** and **Ginger Schnapps:** New liqueur types, inspired by the popularity of peppermint schnapps. (US: **Arrow, DeKuyper**) ⓖ **Ginger-flavored brandy:** Brandy base, 70°, medium-dry. (U.S.: **Arrow, DeKuyper, Leroux, Jacquin**)
	ⓟ **Piment-O-Dram** *(Jamaica):* Medium-sweet liqueur, on a rum base, flavored with allspice, which means hints of clove, cinnamon, and pepper; surprisingly hot, which suggests a measure of chili.
Misc.	Off-the-beaten-track flavors, which are more novelties than commercial products. None has ever been wildly popular, but they may be just the thing to satisfy your palate. ⓟ *Honey:* **Bärenjäger Honey Liqueur** *(Germany)* is one of the rare examples of its type; it tastes much like honey, but the substantial 76° asserts itself in the aftertaste.
	ⓟ *Maple:* **Rieder Maple Liqueur** *(Canada)* is based on maple syrup, and that's what it tastes like.
	ⓟ *Roses:* **Stock Rosolio** *(Italy)* is a reddish liqueur that evokes the scent of rose petals, other fragrant blossoms, and a hint of spice.

FLAVOR SOURCE	DESCRIPTION
Misc. (cont'd)	℗ *Tea:* Currently represented by **Iced Tea** *(U.S.)*, whose name is also an accurate flavor description; **Tiffin** *(Germany)*; and **Suntory Green Tea Liqueur** *(Japan)*, which taste more like strong, brewed, sweetened tea.
	Ⓖ *Violets:* **Parfait Amour** has a lavender-blue color to suggest its violet flavor; however, vanilla and a hint of spice are what come through in this very sweet liqueur. **Crème Yvette** is similar, but has more violet perfume and flavor.
	Ⓖ *Vanilla:* Usually only an accent flavor, it predominates in **Caramella Liqueur** *(U.S.)*, which has a candy taste.

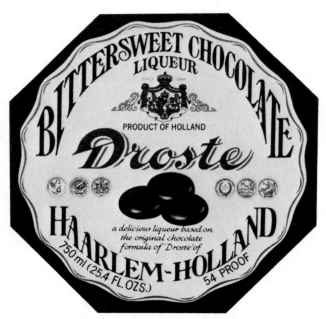

Bittersweet in this instance is something of a misnomer; being a liqueur, the product is sweet. But the Droste name is assurance of honest chocolate flavor.

Liquor-Based Liqueurs

Unlike the majority of liqueurs, which are made on a base of virtually neutral alcohol, each liqueur in this group is based on a specific spirit—whisky, rum, etc. While all are flavored in one way or another, the liquor base adds its own distinctive character to the finished product. As a group, they are fairly alcoholic; most are 80° or higher. All are proprietaries, except as noted.

 LIQUOR-BASED LIQUEURS BUYING GUIDE

FLAVOR SOURCE	DESCRIPTION
Scotch Whisky	**Drambuie** *(Scotland):* Herb-spice blend; hint of honey; Scotch peatiness. **Glayva** *(Scotland):* Herbs and honey; light whisky notes. **Lochan Ora** *(Scotland):* 70°; herbs and honey; Scotch peatiness.
Irish Whiskey	**Irish Mist** *(Ireland):* Honey and whiskey flavors, with definite herbal accents.
American Whiskeys	**Jeremiah Weed** *(U.S.):* Bourbon base, 100°; bourbon flavor with citrus-vanilla notes; fairly sweet and syrupy. **Rock and Rye** *(U.S.):* Generic name for whiskey-based liqueur that contains crystals of rock candy; flavored with fruits and sometimes contains cut-up fruits; 48° to 80°. **Southern Comfort** *(U.S.):* Popularly deemed to be based on bourbon, but bourbon is not apparent in the taste; peach and citrus flavors, with peach in the finish; moderately sweet; often used as a whiskey in southern U.S.; 100°. **Wild Turkey Liqueur** *(U.S.):* Bourbon base; citrus and spice flavors.

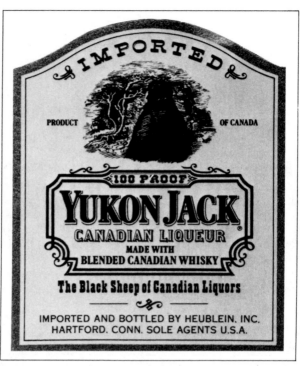

This 100° Canadian liqueur likes to project a macho image. Note the tongue-in-cheek claim that Yukon Jack is "the black sheep of Canadian liqueurs."

FLAVOR SOURCE	DESCRIPTION
Canadian Whisky	**George M. Tiddy's Canadian Liqueur** *(Canada):* Citrus-herb flavors; smooth and sweet; 72°. **Yukon Jack** *(Canada):* Similar flavor to Tiddy's, but whisky character is more evident; 100°.
Rum	**Paso Fino Rum** *(Puerto Rico):* Essentially a sweetened rum; 60°. **Rumona** *(Jamaica):* Honey and spice, plus rum; 63°. **Clément Créole Shrubb** *(Martinique):* Orange and rum flavor; hint of spice in background; smooth, medium-sweet; stylish.

THE LEGENDS OF THE LOST FORMULAS

The oral and recorded history of liqueurs is awash with tales of rare secret formulas that had vanished—sunk without a trace—only to reappear miraculously (and conveniently) centuries later. While these legends do not add much to our wisdom, they are interesting conversational gambits, and only a curmudgeon would delve too deeply into their origins. The following are representative of the genre.

"The masterpiece that is Bénédictine" was created in 1510 by Dom Bernardo Vincelli, a monk of the Benedictine monastery at Fécamp, France. When the abbey was destroyed during the French Revolution, the formula was lost. Seventy-odd years later, it was cunningly reconstructed by one M. Le Grand, who reintroduced the liqueur commercially. An arrangement made with the Order permits use of its name and the initials "D.O.M.", which stands for its maxim, *Deo Optimo Maximo*—to God, most good, most great.

"Chartreuse, the World's Most Mysterious Liqueur" was invented by a 16th-century alchemist who presented it to the Carthusian monks as a "health liqueur." The monks perfected the formula, which became the Maltese Falcon of its day—everyone tried to get hold of it. Despite torture during the French Revolution, the monks did not disclose their secret. Carthusians resumed production in 1817 as a tactic to reunite the order.

"Irish Mist, Ireland's Legendary Liqueur." A thousand years ago, warring clans ruled Ireland and the secret of making "heather wine" was zealously guarded. When Ireland was invaded, the formula, like the country, was lost. In the 19th century, Irish distillers began experimenting, hoping to duplicate the precious recipe. Then, in 1948, an Austrian refugee turned up at a distillery with his family recipe for heather liqueur—known to be of Irish origin. When compounded, it was obviously the ancient "heather wine," and the long search was ended.

"Drambuie: A Link with the '45." After the unsuccessful Scottish rebellion of 1745, Bonnie Prince Charlie (a.k.a. "The Pretender") was given sanctuary by a Captain MacKinnon. As a token of his gratitude, the Prince gave MacKinnon the secret royal recipe for *an dram buidheach*—the drink that satisfies. The MacKinnon family kept the knowledge under their bonnets for ages. In 1906, they finally went public with Drambuie, an anglicized version of the original name. The recipe, however, is still a dark secret.

Cream Liqueurs

This category of liqueurs is the newest to emerge. Born less than 10 years ago, it represents a genuine breakthrough in spiritous beverages. Creams should not be confused with the liqueurs called "Cows," which are made with non-dairy ingredients. Cream liqueurs were first developed in Ireland, but are now being produced in England and other European countries, the U.S., and Australia—and there are more in the blueprint stage.

The primary ingredients are fresh dairy cream and spirits—flavored and sweetened, of course. They are made by a process that combines normally antagonistic elements—cream and spirits—into a harmonious entity that will remain stable under market conditions. The early examples required refrigeration after opening, but the state of the art has made this unnecessary in most cases. However, producers suggest that consumers treat the product "as you would fine wine." A subtle caveat.

Cream liqueurs have the consistency of extra-rich whipping cream, which imparts a smooth, even unctuous mouth feel that is as much a part of the taste experience as the rather unaggressive flavorings. One almost predictable development, incidentally, has been the appearance of several creams that feature the flavor of another runaway best-selling liqueur type—amaretto.

Most are 34°; all are proprietaries.

★   **CREAM LIQUEURS BUYING GUIDE**   ★

BRANDS ▶

Baileys Original Irish Cream *(Ireland):* The one that launched the category; based on Irish spirits; light chocolate flavor with faint perceptions of coconut and coffee.

Baitz Island Cream *(Australia):* Based on Scotch; coconut and chocolate; subtle hint of Scotch smokiness.

Cara Mia *(U.S.):* Amaretto flavored.

Carolans Irish Cream *(Ireland):* Based on Irish spirits with some Irish whiskey; flavored with honey.

Conticream *(Australia):* Some Scotch in the spirit base; comes in either chocolate or coffee flavor.

Cremaretto *(Italy):* Amaretto flavor with hint of chocolate.

Demi-Tasse Coffee Cream Liqueur *(Ireland):* Based on French spirits, including some cognac; coffee flavor; hint of cognac adds complexity.

Droste Cream Liqueur *(U.S.):* Flavored with bittersweet chocolate essence from Holland.

Dunphy's *(U.S.):* Based on Irish spirits. Vanilla is predominant flavor perception.

Emmets *(Ireland):* Based on Irish spirits. Light chocolate with hint of honey.

Greensleeves *(U.K.):* Some brandy in the spirit base; mint flavor, hint of chocolate.

Leroux Irish Cream Liqueur *(Ireland):* Based on Irish spirits; chocolate with vanilla and butterscotch undertones.

Meyer's Original Rum Cream *(Jamaica):* Based on Jamaica rum; has pronounced rum flavor with hints of chocolate, vanilla, and nut.

O'Darby Irish Cream *(Ireland):* Based on Irish whiskey; hint of chocolate.

Venetian Cream *(Italy):* Based on Italian brandy; hints of almond, butterscotch, and coconut.

Waterford Cream *(Ireland):* Based on Irish spirits, rich chocolate; vanilla and almond notes.

Application: While liqueurs are still enjoyed as after-dinner digestifs, they are increasingly accepted as appealing beverages appropriate to a variety of situations and uses—particularly as ingredients in mixed drinks. In fact, the reputation of some liqueurs has been built on their association with a particular cocktail. The examples of Kahlua in the Black Russian, Galliano in the Harvey Wallbanger, and, to a lesser extent, amaretto in the Godfather come to mind in this connection. Even *crème de noyaux*, a little-known liqueur, found new life as an ingredient in the Pink Squirrel, one of many variations on the venerable Alexander cocktail.

The back label of almost every liqueur bottle suggests a variety of uses for the product, and often little booklets offering more helpful hints are draped around these bottles. When not mixed, liqueurs should be poured into goblets large enough to allow appreciation of their voluptuous bouquets; the traditional thimble-size liqueur glasses are to be shunned. Chilling or pouring liqueurs over ice cuts the sweetness a bit, as does adding a splash of vodka, brandy, or soda.

Bear in mind that liqueurs tend to be more perishable than other spirits because of their lower alcohol content and delicate ingredients. Fortunately, most come in half bottles and even sampler sizes, which are useful if you are trying something for the first time.

And for a new entertaining idea, consider a liqueur tasting, with four to six different liqueurs—an interesting alternative to the ubiquitous wine tasting.

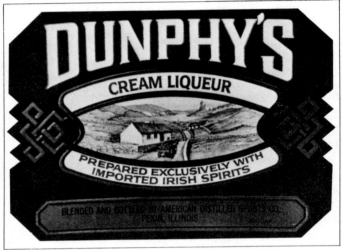

As the label indicates, Dunphy's is made with Irish spirits. But it is bottled in the U.S., using high quality American dairy products.

Care and Handling of Spirits

Because of the amount of alcohol they contain, spirits are far less fragile than wine or beer. Once spirits are bottled and tightly sealed—that is, removed from any contact with air—they remain virtually unchanged for an indefinite time. The only exceptions are certain liqueurs, which are less alcoholic than other spirits and often contain fairly delicate flavoring materials.

To keep all spirits in prime condition, observe these few simple rules:
- Store spirits in an upright position. If a bottle rests on its side for a prolonged period, the alcohol in the spirit may deteriorate the closure.
- Avoid storing bottles in very warm places (e.g., next to a radiator) or in bright light.
- Check the level of the liquid in the neck of any old bottle of spirits. If it appears low, there may have been some leakage or evaporation due to a faulty or deteriorated closure. If the color seems very dark, a faulty closure may have allowed oxidation (from exposure to air) to occur.
- An opened bottle will retain its quality for many months if it is tightly reclosed after each use. Liqueurs, particularly those of low proof, may change color or flavor after a shorter period of time, however. It sometimes helps to store liqueurs of 40° or less in the refrigerator after they have been opened. Storage suggestions are sometimes given on the label.

The High Spirits Quiz

How to rate yourself: 5 correct answers or less means you need work. Read the *Guide* thoroughly, then give it another go. Ten correct answers indicates that you have a solid comprehension of the subject. Riffling through the *Guide* regularly will refine your understanding. If all your answers are correct, you are a perfect "14"—and a bona fide member of the spirits aristocracy.

1. Which of the following alcoholic beverages are distilled spirits? (a) gin (b) brandy (c) rum (d) wine (e) liqueurs (f) whisky

2. True or false: Rye is another name for blended whiskey.

3. Proof is a way of stating the alcoholic content of a spirit. Is the same proof scale or count used everywhere in the world?

4. Does sour mash bourbon taste sour?

5. Scotch whisky and Irish whiskey are both made from barley and other grains. What accounts for the major taste difference between these spirits from the British Isles?

6. What do applejack, slivovitz, mirabelle, and himbeergeist all have in common?

7. True or false: Armagnac is aged cognac.

8. Can you name the spirit that is legally required to be as free as possible from distinctive flavor, aroma, and character?

9. Marc is (a) a liqueur (b) a brandy (c) an aperitif.

10. What is considered to be the first spirit distilled on the American continent?

11. A bottle of 80 proof bourbon is (a) 80% alcohol (b) 100% alcohol (c) 40% alcohol.

12. Should liquor bottles be stored upright or, like wine, horizontally?

13. Scotch is native to Scotland, Canadian is indigenous to Canada, and Irish whiskey comes only from the Emerald Isle. Does the U.S. have a unique spirit?

14. Which of the following are liqueurs? (a) pisco (b) kirsch (c) sambuca (d) quetsch

Answers are on the following pages of the Guide:

1. Page 7	**6.** Page 70	**11.** Page 13
2. Page 43	**7.** Page 57	**12.** Page 139
3. Page 13	**8.** Page 82	**13.** Page 36
4. Page 36	**9.** Page 68	**14.** Page 111
5. Page 33	**10.** Page 35	

Bibliography

Carson, Gerald. *The Social History of Bourbon.* New York: Dodd, Mead & Co., 1963.

Doxat, John. *Stirred—Not Shaken.* London: Hutchinson Benham Ltd., 1976.

Gorman, Marion and Felipe P. de Alba. *The Tequila Book.* Chicago: Contemporary Books, Inc., 1978.

Grossman, Harold J. *Grossman's Guide to Wines, Beers, and Spirits, Sixth Revised Edition,* revised by Harriet Lembeck. New York: Scribners, 1977.

Hallgarten, Peter. *Liqueurs.* London: Wine & Spirit Publications, 1967.

Hannum, Hurst and Robert S. Blumberg. *Brandies and Liqueurs of the World.* New York: Doubleday & Co., 1976.

Lichine, Alexis. *New Encyclopedia of Wines & Spirits.* New York: Alfred A Knopf, 1974.

Lockhart, Sir Robert Bruce. *Scotch.* London: Putnam, 1951.

Lord, Tony. *The World Of Spirits.* New York: Sovereign Books, 1979.

Magee, Malachy. *1000 Years of Irish Whiskey.* Dublin: O'Brien Press, 1980.

Mendelsohn, Oscar. *The Dictionary of Drink and Drinking.* New York: Hawthorn Books, 1965.

White, Francesca. *Cheers!* London: Paddington Press, Ltd., 1977.

INDEX

INDEX